great
gluten-free baking

great gluten-free baking

over 80 delicious cakes and bakes

Louise Blair

hamlyn

First published in Great Britain in 2007 by
Hamlyn, a division of Octopus Publishing Group Ltd.
2–4 Heron Quays, London E14 4JP, UK

ISBN-13: 978-0-600-61633-7
ISBN-10: 0-600-61633-9

A CIP catalogue record for this book is available from the British Library

Printed and bound in China

10 9 8 7 6 5 4 3 2 1

Notes
Ovens should be preheated to the specified temperature.

This book includes dishes made with nuts and nut derivatives. It is advisable for
those with known allergic reactions to nuts and nut derivatives and those who
may be potentially vulnerable to these allergies, such as pregnant and nursing
mothers, invalids, the elderly, babies, and children, to avoid foods made with
nuts. It is also prudent to check the labels of comercially prepared products
for the possible inclusion of nut derivatives.

This book should not be considered a replacement for professional medical
treatment; a physician should be consulted on all matters relating to health.
While the advice and information in this book are believed to be accurate,
neither the author nor the publisher can accept any legal responsibility for
any illness sustained while following the advice in this book.

contents

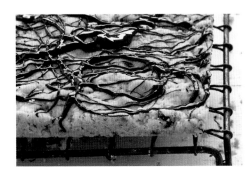

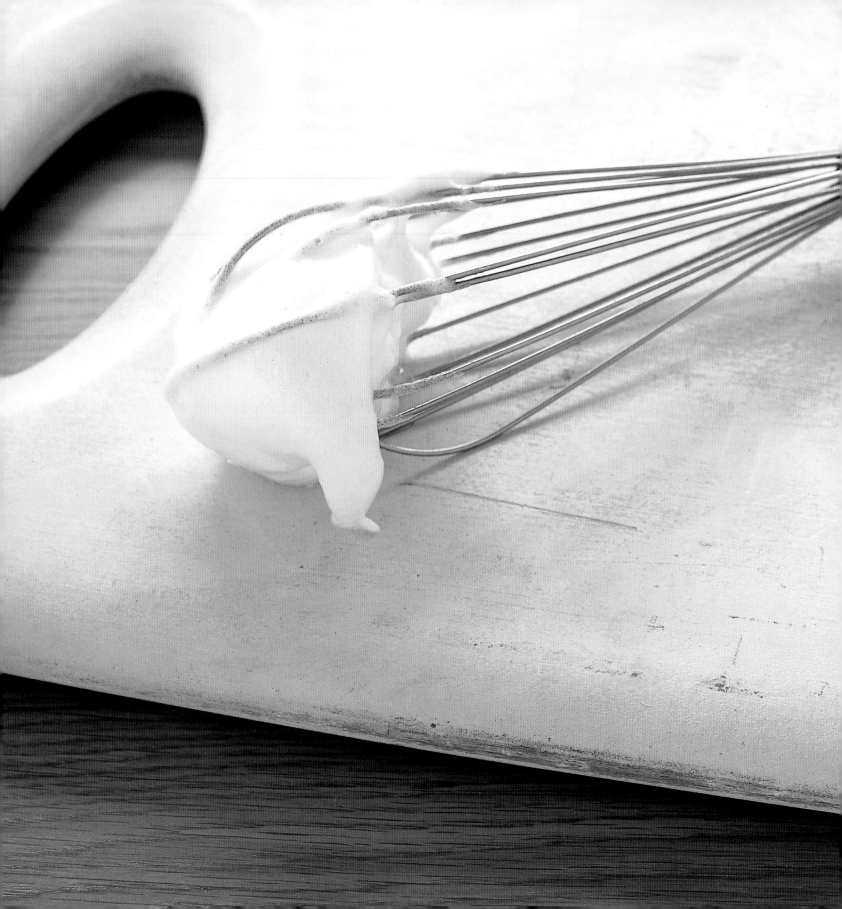

introduction

understanding gluten intolerance and celiac disease

When our ancestors turned from hunting and gathering to agriculture, gluten-containing crops, such as wheat and barley, were cultivated for the first time. Ever since this evolutionary development some people have been unable to tolerate any gluten in their diet. Initially, sufferers were found only among the groups of people who grew these crops, and much of the world's population remained relatively unaffected. Now, however, as populations have migrated and intermingled, the genetic potential for an intolerance to gluten has increased. The condition arising from this gluten intolerance is called celiac disease. Research has now shown that a surprisingly high number of people are affected by the disease.

what is gluten?

Gluten is a type of protein found in wheat, barley, and rye. It makes up about 80 percent of the proteins in wheat. The gluten in wheat is called gliadin; in barley it is hordein and in rye, secalin.

Oats contain a protein that is similar to gluten and which is tolerated by most people with celiac disease. However, because most oats and oat products are contaminated by wheat and barley—either from growing adjacent to these crops and/or from shared milling equipment—it is essential that only pure sources of oats are eaten. You should refer to your healthcare professionals for specific advice about your individual tolerance to oats.

celiac disease

Celiac disease is a chronic inflammatory disease of the lining of the small bowel. It is an autoimmune disease that is caused by intolerance to gluten. When gluten is eaten by people with celiac disease it causes the body's immune system to attack the lining of the gut. The villi (small fingerlike projections in the gut that help with absorption) are destroyed. This reduces the ability of the gut to absorb nutrients from food, which can result in vitamin and mineral deficiencies.

Celiac disease affects one in one hundred people, but because it tends to run in families the risk in families with a history of it is increased to one in ten. People of any age, sex, or ethnicity can be affected: the most common age of diagnosis is 40–50 years old. Left untreated, it can have serious health implications, such as anemia, osteoporosis, and even some forms of cancer.

Symptoms The symptoms of celiac disease range in severity from one person to another. Bowel problems such as diarrhea, constipation, bloating, gas, and nausea can be common and are often confused with irritable bowel syndrome (IBS). Other symptoms include an itchy skin rash called dermatitis herpetiformis; weight loss or failure to gain weight, anemia, tiredness, canker sores, hair loss, and depression. Symptoms of celiac disease are often attributed to stress, resulting in delayed diagnosis or even misdiagnosis. However, it is now possible to diagnose the disease via simple blood tests and by an endoscopy and a biopsy in the jejunal region of the gut.

Treatment The only effective treatment for celiac disease is to avoid eating gluten permanently. The gut of a person with celiac disease has often been damaged, over a long period of time, by ingesting gluten. Fortunately, the damage is reversible. Switching to a lifelong gluten-free diet initiates the gut-healing process and, although this can take up to two years or even longer, most people do start to feel better within just a few weeks.

One drawback to a gluten-free diet is that it can be low in fiber, which can lead to constipation in some people. To avoid this, it is important to eat plenty of high-fiber, gluten-free foods, such as fruit, vegetables, and legumes.

living with gluten intolerance

Having an intolerance to gluten doesn't mean avoiding your favorite foods. It simply means knowing how to avoid the offending grains and their products, most notably flour, and the substitutions you should make. As well as occurring in obvious foods, such as bread, cookies, cakes, pastries, and pasta, it is used in a variety of processed foods, some of them surprising, such as tomato sauce, mustard, soups, and flavored potato chips. Although wheat flour is found in many everyday foods, there are plenty of alternatives nowadays made with gluten-free ingredients. Gluten-free flour and other gluten-free ingredients (see pages 10–13) are available from health-food stores, and some ingredients, such as rice flour, can be found in grocery stores. These ensure gluten-free baking is not only possible, but easy and delicious, as the recipes in this book demonstrate.

gluten-free baking

Making cakes, cookies, bread, and pastry without using wheat flour is perfectly possible. There are many gluten-free baking ingredients available—from health-food stores, organic food stores, mail-order companies, and grocery stores—so don't be afraid to try your hand at some gluten-free baking. Flour aside, many ingredients used in baking are naturally gluten-free, for example milk, eggs, butter, margarine, sugar, fruit, nuts, seeds, vegetables, and most preserves and spreads.

using flour

For a gluten-free diet, you need to avoid all types of wheat, barley, and rye flours. The baking qualities of gluten-free flours are different from wheat flour, so there may be some trial and error involved while you become accustomed to cooking with them.

Gluten-free flours are made from corn, rice, potato, soy, chestnut, buckwheat, millet, garbanzo (also called chickpea, gram, or channa), tapioca, or sorghum. You can also use commercial flour mixes made from a combination of gluten-free ingredients.

Baking without gluten is challenging because removing gluten from flour reduces its elasticity. However, there are some ingredients that can help.

Mix and match gluten-free flours for great results

Xanthan gum Xanthan gum (also known as E415) is a type of starch that is useful in gluten-free baking because it replaces the "stretch factor" of gluten, thereby helping gluten-free flours to bind in a way more similar to wheat flour. Xanthan gum comes as a powder and needs to be combined with the gluten-free flour mix before any liquid is added. It can be purchased from health-food stores.

Guar gum This is a gum derived from the seeds of the locust bean, which acts as a thickening and bulking agent.

shopping for gluten-free ingredients

Not only is home cooking satisfying and usually more tasty than store-bought products, you'll be confident in the knowledge that your cooking is completely gluten-free as long as you take care when choosing your ingredients. For example, garbanzo flour (made from chickpeas) is naturally gluten-free, but it may have been contaminated by traces of gluten-containing wheat flour if milled in the same place or stored in the same containers. It's therefore important to buy reputable brands that can guarantee their products are safe and free from gluten contamination. Manufacturers now have to list all the ingredients in their products on the food label, so you can avoid foods that are unsuitable because gluten-containing ingredients will be clearly labeled.

Just as with standard manufactured foods, the taste and texture of gluten-free foods varies from one brand to another, so shop around until you discover the ones that you like. There are a number of gluten-free food manufacturers and no shortage of information on them and their products on the Internet. Many offer a mail order service so you can still buy gluten-free foods even if you can't find the products in your local stores. There's simply no excuse not to buy gluten-free ingredients and get baking! Have fun with the recipes in this book and enjoy making and eating gluten-free cakes, muffins, cookies, and breads.

muffins
and more

orange and pistachio butterfly cakes

Orange and pistachio go together well in these flavorsome cakes.

Makes 12 cakes
Preparation time 10 minutes
Cooking time 15 minutes

1 cup rice flour
2 teaspoons gluten-free baking powder
8 teaspoons (1 stick) butter, softened
½ cup granulated sugar
3 tablespoons unsalted pistachios, ground
2 large eggs
grated rind and juice 1 orange
4 tablespoons gluten-free orange curd

Nutritional information:
Cal 196 (819 kJ) Protein 3 g Carb 23 g
Fat 10 g Saturated fat 6 g Fiber 1 g

1 Preheat the oven to 400°F. Line a 12-hole muffin pan with paper liners. Place all the ingredients apart from the orange curd in a food processor and whiz until smooth, or beat together in a large bowl.

2 Divide the mixture between the paper liners and place in the preheated oven for 12–15 minutes, until golden and firm to the touch. Remove the cakes from the oven and transfer to a wire rack to cool.

3 Cut the top off each cake to create a level surface, and save the 12 tops. Spread each top with a little orange curd, then cut it in half and place it on a cake at an angle to resemble butterfly wings.

date and pecan muffins

The dates provide a richness of flavor and the pecans a satisfying crunch, making these muffins delicious.

Makes 18 muffins
Preparation time 10 minutes
Cooking time 20 minutes

½ cup pitted dates, chopped
2 teaspoons baking soda
2 tablespoons boiling water
2½ cups brown rice flour
1 tablespoon gluten-free baking powder
½ cup packed dark brown sugar
1 cup pecans, roughly chopped
8 tablespoons (1 stick) butter, melted
4 eggs, beaten
1¼ cups buttermilk
2 tablespoons milk
2 tablespoons light brown sugar

Nutritional information:
Cal 212 (886 kJ) Protein 6 g Carb 25 g
Fat 10 g Saturated fat 4 g Fiber 3 g

1 Preheat the oven to 400°F. Line two large 12-hole muffin pans with 18 large paper liners. Place the dates, baking soda, and water in a bowl and set aside for 10 minutes.

2 Meanwhile, in a large bowl, mix together the flour, baking powder, dark brown sugar, and pecans. In another bowl, mix together the butter, eggs, buttermilk, and milk, then pour this into the dry mixture along with the dates and their liquid. Quickly stir just to combine all the ingredients roughly.

3 Spoon the mixture into the muffin pans, sprinkle over a little light brown sugar, and place in the preheated oven for 15–20 minutes, until golden and risen. Remove the muffins from the oven and transfer to a wire rack to cool.

lavender cupcakes

The lavender makes these little cakes perfect for sophisticated afternoon entertaining.

Makes 12 cakes
Preparation time 10 minutes
Cooking time 15 minutes

1 tablespoon milk
1 teaspoon lavender flowers (small, individual flower heads, removed from the stalk)
½ cup granulated sugar
8 tablespoons (1 stick) butter, softened
⅔ cup rice flour
1 tablespoon garbanzo (chickpea) flour
2 eggs, beaten
2 tablespoons ground almonds
1 teaspoon gluten-free baking powder
1 teaspoon xanthan gum

for the decoration
1 cup confectioners' sugar
12 small lavender heads

Nutritional information:
Cal 185 (773 kJ) Protein 2 g Carb 27 g
Fat 8 g Saturated fat 5 g Fiber 1 g

1 Preheat the oven to 350°F. Line a 12-hole muffin pan with paper liners. Place the milk and lavender in a small bowl, cover with plastic wrap, and microwave on full power for 10 seconds. Remove and let stand for 10 minutes to let the flavors develop.

2 Place all the cake ingredients, including the lavender-infused milk, in a food processor and whiz until smooth, or beat together in a large bowl.

3 Spoon the mixture into the paper liners and place in the preheated oven for 12–15 minutes, until golden and just firm to the touch. Remove the cakes from the oven and transfer to a wire rack to cool.

4 Add a few drops of water to the confectioners' sugar—just enough to form a stiff frosting. Smooth a little over each cake and decorate with a lavender head.

plum and polenta muffins

These unusual muffins are great for picnics
or afternoon snacks.

Makes 12 muffins
Preparation time 20 minutes
Cooking time 20 minutes

4 small, ripe plums, stoned and
   roughly chopped
1 cup packed light brown sugar
5 tablespoons brown rice flour
6 tablespoons corn flour
2 teaspoons gluten-free baking powder
1 teaspoon xanthan gum
1 teaspoon ground cinnamon
½ cup plus 1½ tablespoons polenta
2 eggs, beaten
few drops vanilla extract
6 tablespoons butter, melted
1 cup buttermilk

Nutritional information:
Cal 227 (949 kJ) Protein 4 g Carb 33 g
Fat 9 g Saturated fat 4 g Fiber 1 g

1 Preheat the oven to 350°F. Line a large 12-hole muffin pan with large paper liners. Place the plums in a bowl, sprinkle over a little of the sugar, and set aside for 10 minutes, until the juices begin to ooze.

2 Meanwhile, place all the dry ingredients in a large bowl and stir together. Combine the eggs, vanilla extract, butter, and buttermilk in another bowl, then stir this into the dry ingredients along with the plums and any juices.

3 Spoon the mixture into the paper liners and place in the preheated oven for 20 minutes, until risen and golden. Remove the muffins from the oven and transfer to a wire rack to cool.

white chocolate and apricot muffins

Melting white chocolate combined with soft apricots
is delectable, so these muffins won't last long.

Makes 15 muffins
Preparation time 10 minutes
Cooking time 20 minutes

½ cup dried apricots, chopped
grated rind and juice 1 orange
2½ cups brown rice flour
1 teaspoon baking soda
2 teaspoons gluten-free baking powder
1 cup granulated sugar
3 ounces gluten-free white chocolate,
  chopped
6 tablespoons butter, melted
4 eggs, beaten
1¼ cups buttermilk

Nutritional information:
Cal 227 (949 kJ) **Protein** 4 g **Carb** 33 g
Fat 9 g **Saturated fat** 6 g **Fiber** 2 g

1 Preheat the oven to 350°F. Line two large 12-hole muffin pans
with 15 large paper liners. Place the apricots and the orange rind
and juice in a small saucepan, bring to a boil, and simmer gently for
5 minutes, then set aside.

2 Meanwhile, sift the flour, baking soda, and baking powder
together into a large bowl. Add the sugar and chocolate and stir
together. Mix together the wet ingredients and the soaked apricots,
and fold them roughly into the dry mixture.

3 Spoon the mixture into the paper liners and and place in the
preheated oven for 20 minutes, until risen and golden. Remove
the muffins from the oven and transfer to a wire rack to cool.

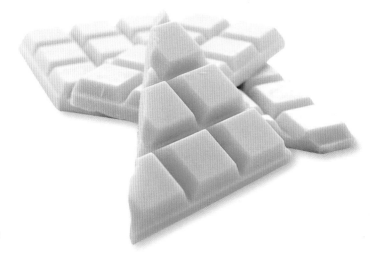

lemon and raspberry cupcakes

These luscious melt-in-the-mouth cakes combine the sweetness of raspberries with the sharpness of lemon.

Makes 12 cakes
Preparation time 10 minutes
Cooking time 15 minutes

10 tablespoons (1¼ sticks) butter, softened
⅔ cup granulated sugar
½ cup rice flour
½ cup corn flour
1 tablespoon gluten-free baking powder
grated rind and juice 1 lemon
3 eggs, beaten
1 cup raspberries
1 tablespoon gluten-free lemon curd

Nutritional information:
Cal 206 (861 kJ) Protein 3 g Carb 22 g
Fat 12 g Saturated fat 7 g Fiber 1 g

1 Preheat the oven to 400°F. Line a large 12-hole muffin pan with large paper liners. Place all the ingredients except the raspberries and the lemon curd in a large bowl and whisk together using an electric mixer, or beat with a wooden spoon. Fold in the raspberries.

2 Spoon half of the mixture into the paper liners, dot over a little lemon curd, then add the remaining sponge mixture. Place in the preheated oven for 12–15 minutes, until golden and firm to the touch. Remove the cakes from the oven and transfer to a wire rack to cool.

chocolate zucchini muffins

Grated zucchini are the secret to keeping these muffins light and moist.

Makes 12 muffins
Preparation time 10 minutes
Cooking time 20 minutes

2 medium zucchini, grated
2 eggs, beaten
½ cup vegetable oil
½ cup granulated sugar
½ cup dried dates, chopped
2 tablespoons milk
¾ cup corn flour
¾ cup brown rice flour
2 tablespoons cocoa powder
1 teaspoon xanthan gum
2 teaspoons gluten-free baking powder

for the frosting (if desired)
1 cup quark
1 tablespoon confectioners' sugar
grated rind 1 orange
few toasted chopped nuts (optional)

Nutritional information:
Cal 223 (932 kJ) Protein 7 g Carb 28 g
Fat 10 g Saturated fat 2 g Fiber 2 g

SHOWN ON PAGES 14–15

1 Preheat the oven to 350°F. Line a large 12-hole muffin pan with large paper liners. (If you use colored liners as pictured on pages 14–15, the dark muffin will show through, so you can achieve a particularly attractive effect if you line each hole with two or more colored cases.) Place the zucchini, eggs, oil, sugar, dates, and milk in a large bowl and stir together. In a separate bowl, sift together the dry ingredients, then quickly and roughly stir them into the wet ingredients.

2 Divide the mixture between the paper liners and place in the preheated oven for about 20 minutes, until risen and firm to the touch. Remove the muffins from the oven and transfer to a wire rack to cool.

3 For a special treat, place the quark, confectioners' sugar, and orange rind in a bowl and beat together, then smooth the frosting over the muffins. Sprinkle with a few nuts, if using.

cranberry and orange cupcakes

With their seasonal flavors, these little cakes are
a great treat at Christmastime.

Makes 12 cakes
Preparation time 10 minutes
Cooking time 15 minutes

1 cup dried cranberries
grated rind and juice 1 orange
10 tablespoons (1¼ sticks) butter,
    softened
¾ cup granulated sugar
½ cup rice flour
½ cup corn flour
1 tablespoon gluten-free baking powder
2 tablespoons milk
3 eggs, beaten

for the frosting
1¾ cups confectioners' sugar
grated rind and juice 1 small orange

Nutritional information:
Cal 265 (1108 kJ) **Protein** 4 g **Carb** 36 g
Fat 12 g **Saturated fat** 7 g **Fiber** 2 g

1 Preheat the oven to 400°F. Line a 12-hole muffin pan with paper liners. Place the cranberries and orange rind and juice in a small pan, bring to a boil then simmer gently for 5 minutes.

2 Meanwhile, place the remaining cake ingredients in a food processor and whiz until smooth (or beat together in a large bowl). Add the cranberries and any juice and stir the ingredients together, then spoon into the paper liners. Place in the preheated oven for 12–15 minutes, until golden and risen. Remove the cakes from the oven and transfer to a wire rack to cool.

3 In a small bowl, mix together the confectioners' sugar, grated rind, and enough orange juice to make a thickish frosting. Smooth a little over the cakes and let set.

cherry crumble muffins

Juicy cherries keep these muffins really moist, while the crumble topping adds some crunch.

Makes 12 muffins
Preparation time 10 minutes
Cooking time 20 minutes

1½ cups brown rice flour
1 teaspoon baking soda
2 teaspoon gluten-free baking powder
½ cup granulated sugar
10-ounce can black cherries, drained
6 tablespoons butter, melted
2 eggs, beaten
⅔ cup buttermilk

for the crumbly topping
1 tablespoon ground almonds
1 tablespoon light brown sugar
1 tablespoon brown rice flour
1 tablespoon butter

Nutritional information:
Cal 189 (790 kJ) Protein 3 g Carb 27 g
Fat 8 g Saturated fat 5 g Fiber 1 g

1 Preheat the oven to 350°F. Line a large 12-hole muffin pan with large paper liners. Sift the flour, baking soda, and baking powder together in a large bowl, then stir in the sugar.

2 In a separate bowl, mix together the cherries, butter, eggs, and buttermilk. Gently combine the dry and wet ingredients, then spoon the mixture into the paper liners.

3 Quickly rub together the topping ingredients and sprinkle over the muffin mixture, then place the muffins in the preheated oven for 20 minutes, until golden and risen. Remove the muffins from the oven and cool on a wire rack.

tiramisu cupcakes

The combination of coffee and marsala provides a
taste of Italy in these little cakes.

Makes 12 cakes
Preparation time 10 minutes
Cooking time 15 minutes

10 tablespoons (1¼ sticks) butter,
  softened
⅔ **cup granulated sugar**
½ **cup rice flour**
½ **cup corn flour**
1 tablespoon cocoa powder
1 tablespoon gluten-free baking powder
1 teaspoon instant espresso coffee
2 tablespoons milk
3 eggs, beaten

for the topping
1 cup mascarpone cheese
2 tablespoons confectioners' sugar
1 tablespoon marsala

Nutritional information:
Cal 276 (1154 kJ) Protein 4 g Carb 21 g
Fat 20 g Saturated fat 12 g Fiber 1 g

1 Preheat the oven to 400°F. Line a 12-hole muffin pan with paper liners. Place all the cake ingredients in a food processor and whiz until smooth, or beat together in a large bowl.

2 Spoon the mixture into the paper liners and and place in the preheated oven for 12–15 minutes, until risen. Remove the cakes from the oven and transfer to a wire rack to cool.

3 Place the topping ingredients in a bowl and beat together, then smooth a little mixture over each cake.

coconut cupcakes

These are really moist and flavorsome—delicious
with a cup of coffee or tea at any time of day.

Makes 12 cakes
Preparation time 10 minutes
Cooking time 15 minutes

12 tablespoons (1½ sticks) butter,
 softened
¾ cup granulated sugar
few drops vanilla extract
3 eggs, beaten
¾ cup brown rice flour
¾ cup corn flour
2 teaspoons gluten-free baking powder
½ cup shredded coconut, soaked in ½
 cup boiling water

for the topping
4 tablespoons butter, softened
1 cup confectioners' sugar
2 tablespoons shredded coconut,
 toasted

Nutritional information:
Cal 323 (1350 kJ) Protein 2 g Carb 37 g
Fat 19 g Saturated fat 13 g Fiber 1 g

1 Preheat the oven to 350°F. Line a 12-hole muffin pan with paper liners. Place all the cake ingredients in a food processor and whiz until smooth, or beat together in a large bowl.

2 Spoon the mixture into the paper liners and place in the preheated oven for 12–15 minutes, until golden and risen. Remove the cakes from the oven and transfer to a wire rack to cool.

3 Place the butter and confectioners' sugar in a bowl and beat together until pale and creamy, then stir in the toasted coconut. Spread a little frosting on each cake.

scrumptious strawberry biscuits

No one would guess that these light and airy
biscuits are gluten free.

Makes 8 biscuits
Preparation time 10 minutes
Cooking time 12 minutes

1 cup rice flour, plus a little extra
   for dusting
¾ cup potato flour
1 teaspoon xanthan gum
1 teaspoon gluten-free baking powder
1 teaspoon baking soda
6 tablespoons butter, cubed
3 tablespoons granulated sugar
1 large egg, beaten
3 tablespoons buttermilk, plus a little
   extra for brushing

for the filling
⅔ cup heavy cream
1⅔ cups strawberries, lightly crushed

Nutritional information:
Cal 292 (1221 kJ) Protein 5 g Carb 30 g
Fat 17 g Saturated fat 10 g Fiber 2 g

1 Preheat the oven to 425°F. Place the flours, xanthan gum, baking powder, baking soda, and butter in a food processor and whiz until the mixture resembles fine bread crumbs, or rub in by hand in a large bowl. Stir in the sugar. Using the blade of a knife, stir in the egg and buttermilk until the mixture comes together.

2 Tip the dough out onto a surface dusted lightly with rice flour, and gently press it down to a thickness of 1 inch. Using a 2-inch cutter, cut out eight biscuits. Place on a lightly floured baking sheet, brush with a little buttermilk, then place in the preheated oven for about 12 minutes, until golden and risen. Remove the biscuits from the oven and transfer to a wire rack to cool.

3 Meanwhile, whisk the cream until it forms fairly firm peaks, and fold the strawberries into it. Split the biscuits in half and fill with the strawberry cream. These biscuits are best served on the day they are cooked, preferably still just warm.

moist orange cupcakes

Use lemon in place of orange in these cupcakes if you prefer a stronger citrus taste.

Makes 18 cupcakes
Preparation time 10 minutes
Cooking time 15 minutes

14 tablespoons (1¾ sticks) butter, softened
1 cup granulated sugar
3 eggs, beaten
¼ cup brown rice flour
1¾ cups ground almonds
grated rind and juice 1 orange
½ cup flaked almonds

Nutritional information:
Cal 225 (940 kJ) **Protein** 4 g **Carb** 12 g
Fat 18 g **Saturated fat** 7 g **Fiber** 1 g

1 Preheat the oven to 350°F. Line two mini 12-hole muffin pans with 18 mini paper liners. Place the butter and sugar in a large bowl and beat together until pale and creamy. Gradually beat in the eggs, then fold the flour, ground almonds, and orange rind and juice into the mixture.

2 Spoon the mixture into the paper liners, sprinkle over the almonds, and place in the preheated oven for 12–15 minutes, until golden and risen. Remove the muffins from the oven and transfer to a wire rack to cool.

bite-sized mince pies

The cream cheese in these mini mince pies makes them wonderfully moist.

Makes 18 pies
Preparation time 15 minutes, plus chilling
Cooking time 15 minutes

½ cup polenta
½ cup rice flour, plus a little extra for dusting
½ teaspoon xanthan gum
a pinch allpice
grated rind 1 lemon or orange
7 tablespoons butter
1 tablespoon granulated sugar
1 egg, beaten
a little milk for brushing
a little confectioners' sugar for dusting

for the filling
16-ounce jar gluten-free mince pie filling
½ cup cream cheese

Nutritional information:
Cal 122 (510 kJ) Protein 1 g Carb 16 g
Fat 6 g Saturated fat 4 g Fiber 1 g

1 Place the polenta, flour, xanthan gum, allspice, lemon rind, butter, and sugar in a food processor and whiz until it resembles fine bread crumbs, or rub in by hand in a large bowl. Add the egg and gently mix in, using a knife, adding a little cold water if the mixture is too dry. Bring the mixture together to form a ball, wrap tightly, and chill for 30 minutes.

2 Preheat the oven to 400°F. Remove the pastry from the refrigerator and knead it on a surface dusted lightly with rice flour to soften it a little. Then roll it out thinly and cut out 2-inch rounds and the same number of slightly smaller lids. Use the larger circles to line 18 holes in two 12-hole mini tart pans.

3 Spoon a little mince pie filling and a little cream cheese onto each pie crust base, brush the rim of the lids with milk so they stick to the bases, and put them in place, pressing lightly to seal. Brush the tops with a little extra milk and place in the preheated oven for 12–15 minutes, until golden. Remove the pies from the oven and transfer to a wire rack to cool a little, then serve warm, dusted with confectioners' sugar.

perfect pecan pies

The ideal entertaining dessert! Serve with whipped cream or some gluten-free ice cream for a treat.

Makes 8 pies
Preparation time 15 minutes, plus chilling
Cooking time 20 minutes

½ cup brown rice flour, plus a little extra for dusting
5 tablespoons garbanzo flour
½ cup polenta
1 teaspoon xanthan gum
8 tablespoons (1 stick) butter, cubed
2 tablespoons granulated sugar
1 egg, beaten

for the filling
½ cup packed light brown sugar
10 tablespoons (1¼ sticks) butter
5 tablespoons honey
1⅔ cups pecan halves, half of them roughly chopped
2 eggs, beaten

Nutritional information:
Cal 606 (2533 kJ) Protein 7 g Carb 43 g
Fat 46 g Saturated fat 21 g Fiber 2 g

1 Place the flours, polenta, xanthan gum, and butter in a food processor and whiz until the mixture resembles fine bread crumbs, or rub in by hand in a large bowl. Stir in the sugar. Add the egg and gently mix in, using a knife, adding enough cold water (probably a couple of teaspoons) to make a dough. Try not to let it become too wet. Knead for a few minutes, then wrap closely in plastic wrap and chill for about an hour.

2 Meanwhile, place the sugar, butter and honey for the filling in a medium saucepan and heat until the sugar has dissolved. Let cool for 10 minutes.

3 Preheat the oven to 400°F. While the filling is cooling, remove the dough from the refrigerator and knead it on a surface dusted lightly with rice flour to soften it a little. Divide the dough into eight, then roll each piece out to a thickness of ⅛ inch. Use to line eight individual 4½-inch pie pans, rolling the rolling pin over the top to cut off the excess dough.

4 Stir the chopped pecans and eggs into the filling mixture and pour into the pie crust-lined pans. Arrange the pecan halves over the top, then place the pans in the preheated oven for 15–20 minutes, until the filling is firm. Remove the pies and let cool.

banoffee bites

The popular combination of banana and toffee makes these little cakes absolutely delicious!

Makes 24 bites
Preparation time 10 minutes
Cooking time 12 minutes

1¼ cups brown rice flour
6 tablespoons butter, softened
6 tablespoons granulated sugar
2 teaspoons gluten-free baking powder
1 large banana, mashed
2 eggs
6 toffees, chopped

for the topping
2 tablespoons dried banana slices
1 tablespoon light brown sugar

Nutritional information:
Cal 122 (510 kJ) **Protein** 1 g **Carb** 16 g
Fat 6 g **Saturated fat** 4 g **Fiber** 1 g

1 Preheat the oven to 400°F. Line two 12-hole mini muffin pans with paper liners. Place all the cake ingredients except the toffees in a food processor and whiz until smooth, or beat together in a large bowl. Stir in the toffees.

2 Spoon the mixture into the paper liners, sprinkle over most of the brown sugar and place in the preheated oven for 10–12 minutes, until golden and just firm to the touch. Remove the cakes from the oven and cool on a wire rack. Top with the dried banana slices and sprinkle with the remaining sugar, if you like.

family
favorites

blueberry and apple cake

This moist upside-down cake is so easy to make and is delicious served with a little whipped cream.

Serves 12
Preparation time 10 minutes
Cooking time 1 hour

2 small dessert apples, peeled, cored, and sliced
1 cup (2 sticks) butter, softened
1¼ cups granulated sugar
1½ cups rice flour
1 tablespoon gluten-free baking powder
4 eggs
1 cup blueberries

Nutritional information:
Cal 312 (1304 kJ) **Protein** 5 g **Carb** 35 g
Fat 17 g **Saturated fat** 11 g **Fiber** 2 g

1 Preheat the oven to 400°F. Grease and line the base of a 9-inch springform deep cake pan. Layer the apples over the base of the cake pan.

2 Place the butter, sugar, flour, baking powder, and eggs in a food processor and whiz for 30 seconds, or until well combined; or beat together in a large bowl. Add the blueberries and whiz for 5 seconds, until roughly chopped, or stir until mixed well.

3 Spoon the mixture over the apples. Place in the preheated oven for 50–60 minutes, until golden and just firm to the touch. Remove the cake from the oven, cool for 10 minutes in the pan, then turn out onto a wire rack and let cool completely.

chocolate hazelnut cake

This light and airy cake is also good served as a dessert with a scoop of ice cream or whipped cream.

Serves 12
Preparation time 15 minutes
Cooking time 40 minutes

2 cups blanched hazelnuts
6 eggs, separated
2 cups confectioners' sugar, sifted
1½ cup gluten-free, fresh bread crumbs
1 tablespoon cocoa powder
grated rind and juice 1 orange
6 tablespoons butter, melted

Nutritional information:
Cal 295 (1233 kJ) Protein 7 g Carb 22 g
Fat 20 g Saturated fat 5 g Fiber 2 g

1 Preheat the oven to 350°F. Grease and line a 9-inch deep springform pan. Place the hazelnuts on a baking sheet and cook in the preheated oven for 10 minute,s until golden. Let cool a little, then place in a food processor or liquidizer and whiz until they resemble fine bread crumbs.

2 Place the egg whites in a large clean bowl and whisk until they form stiff peaks. Add 2 tablespoons of the confectioners' sugar and continue to whisk until thick.

3 Place the egg yolks in a separate bowl with the remaining confectioners' sugar and whisk until pale. Fold in the remaining ingredients, including the egg whites, then transfer to the prepared pan. Place in the oven for 40 minutes, then remove the cake from the oven and transfer to a wire rack to cool.

coconut and mango cake

This delicious tropical-inspired cake is great for summer entertaining.

Serves 12
Preparation time 10 minutes
Cooking time 50 minutes

7 tablespoons butter, softened
⅓ cup packed light brown sugar
4 eggs, separated
1¾ cups buttermilk
1¼ cups polenta
1¼ cups rice flour
2 teaspoons gluten-free baking powder
½ cup coconut milk powder
½ cup shredded coconut
flesh 1 ripe mango, pureed

for the filling
1 cup mascarpone cheese
flesh 1 ripe mango, finely chopped
2 tablespoons confectioners' sugar

Nutritional information:
Cal 374 (1563 kJ) Protein 9 g Carb 37 g
Fat 22 g Saturated fat 13 g Fiber 3 g

1 Preheat the oven to 400°F. grease and line a 9-inch round, deep cake pan. Place the butter and sugar in a large bowl and beat until light and fluffy, then beat in the egg yolks, buttermilk, polenta, baking powder, coconut milk powder, and shredded coconut. In a large, clean bowl, whisk the egg whites until they form soft peaks, then fold into the cake mixture with the pureed mango.

2 Spoon the mixture into the prepared pan and place in the preheated oven for 45–50 minutes, until golden and firm to the touch. Remove the cake from the oven and transfer to a wire rack to cool.

3 When the cake is cool, slice it in half. Place the filling ingredients in a bowl and beat together. Use half the filling to sandwich the cake together then smooth the remaining mixture over the top.

fudgy apple loaf

Gooey fudge and moist apple makes this loaf
a real family favorite.

Serves 12
Preparation time 25 minutes
Cooking time 1½ hours

1 cup granulated sugar
3 eggs
2½ cups brown rice flour
1 teaspoon gluten-free baking powder
14 tablespoons (1¾ sticks) butter,
   melted
few drops vanilla extract
2 dessert apples, peeled, cored, and
   chopped

for the fudge
13-ounce can condensed milk
⅔ cup milk
2 cups packed light brown sugar
7 tablespoons butter

Nutritional information:
Cal 376 (1572 kJ) Protein 2 g Carb 57 g
Fat 16 g Saturated fat 11 g Fiber 0 g

1 To make the fudge, place all the ingredients in a heavy-based
saucepan, heat gently until the sugar has dissolved, bring to a
boil, and boil for about 10 minutes, until the mixture reaches 230°F
on a sugar thermometer. Remove from the heat and beat for
5 minutes, then pour into a pan and set aside to cool.

2 Preheat the oven to 350°F. Grease and line a 2-pound loaf pan.
Place the sugar and eggs in a large bowl and whisk together
until pale and thick. Sift the flour and baking powder into the
mixture together, then fold it in with the butter, vanilla extract,
two-thirds of the apple, and three-fourths of the fudge, chopped.
Spoon into the prepared pan, then scatter over the remaining apple
and chopped fudge.

3 Place in the preheated oven for about 1½ hours, until golden and
firm to touch. Remove the cake from the oven and transfer to a
wire rack to cool.

orange and honey cake

This is great to take on a picnic and serve with some fresh fruit or berries.

Serves 10
Preparation time 10 minutes
Cooking time 1 hour

10 tablespoons (1¼ sticks) butter,
    softened
1 cup granulated sugar
grated rind and juice 1 orange
2 tablespoons clear honey
3 tablespoons marmalade
3 eggs, beaten
⅔ cup brown rice flour
1 teaspoon gluten-free baking powder
½ cup polenta

Nutritional information:
Cal 270 (1129 kJ) Protein 1 g Carb 41 g
Fat 12 g Saturated fat 8 g Fiber 1 g

1 Preheat the oven to 325°F. Grease and line an 8-inch square, deep baking pan. Place the butter and sugar in a large bowl, then beat until light and fluffy. Whisk together the orange rind and juice, honey, marmalade, and eggs, then beat into the creamed butter mixture, adding a little of the flour if the mixture curdles.

2 Stir in the remaining ingredients, then spoon into the prepared pan and place in the preheated oven for about 1 hour, until just firm in the middle. Remove the cake from the oven and transfer to a wire rack to cool.

chocolate and chestnut roulade

The flavors of chocolate and chestnut work so well together in this delicious cake.

Serves 8
Preparation time 15 minutes
Cooking time 20 minutes

6 eggs, separated
½ cup granulated sugar
2 tablespoons cocoa powder
confectioners' sugar, for dusting

for the filling
⅔ cup heavy cream, whipped
½ cup chestnut puree or sweetened
   chestnut spread

Nutritional information:
Cal 215 (899 kJ) **Protein** 6 g **Carb** 21 g
Fat 12 g **Saturated fat** 3 g **Fiber** 1 g

1 Preheat the oven to 350°F. Grease and line an 11½ x 7-inch jelly roll pan. Place the egg whites in a large clean bowl and whisk until they form soft peaks. Place the egg yolks and sugar in a separate bowl and whisk together until thick and pale. Fold in the cocoa powder and the egg whites, then tip into the prepared pan.

2 Place in the preheated oven for 20 minutes, then remove from the oven and cool in the pan. Tip out onto a piece of wax paper that has been dusted with confectioners' sugar.

3 Place the cream in a large clean bowl and whisk until it forms soft peaks. Fold the chestnut puree or sweetened chestnut spread into the cream, then smooth the mixture over the roulade.

4 Using the wax paper to help you, carefully roll up the roulade from one short end and lift it gently onto its serving dish. (Don't worry if it cracks—it won't detract from its appearance or taste.) Dust with extra confectioners' sugar. Chill until needed and eat on the day it is made.

butterscotch layer cake

Impress friends and family with this simple but delicious sponge cake.

Serves 10
Preparation time 10 minutes
Cooking time 25 minutes

1 cup (2 sticks) unsalted butter, softened
1 cup granulated sugar
4 eggs
1½ cups rice flour
1 tablespoon gluten-free baking powder
2 tablespoons milk

for the filling
1¼ cups quark
1 cup dulce de leche

Nutritional information:
Cal 444 (1856 kJ) **Protein** 11 g **Carb** 51 g
Fat 22 g **Saturated fat** 13 g **Fiber** 1 g

1 Preheat the oven to 400°F. Grease two 8-inch cake pans. Place all the cake ingredients in a food processor and whiz until smooth, or beat together in a large bowl. Spoon into the prepared pans and place in a preheated oven for 20–25 minutes, until golden and just firm to the touch. Remove the cakes from the oven and transfer to a wire rack to cool.

2 Place the quark and dulce de leche in a bowl and beat together. Use half the mixture to sandwich the cakes together and half for the topping. Eat on the same day, or keep chilled for up to 2 days.

moist almond cake

Ground almonds give this cake a great texture and flavor.

Serves 10
Preparation time 10 minutes
Cooking time 1 hour 50 minutes

2 large oranges
1 cup granulated sugar
2¼ cups ground almonds
1 teaspoon gluten-free baking powder
6 eggs
1¼ cups brown rice flour

Nutritional information:
Cal 371 (1551 kJ) **Protein** 12 g **Carb** 41 g
Fat 18 g **Saturated fat** 2 g **Fiber** 4 g

1 Preheat the oven to 350°F. Grease an 8-inch round, deep cake pan. Place the oranges in a large pan of water, bring to a boil, and simmer gently for 1 hour. Then remove the oranges from the pan, place in a food processor or liquidizer, and blend until pulpy. Remove any obvious pips.

2 Add the remaining ingredients and blend until smooth, then pour into the prepared pan and place in the preheated oven for 45–50 minutes, until just firm to touch. Remove the cake from the oven and transfer to a wire rack to cool. Serve with whipped cream, if you want.

chocolate and rum cake

This may not be a good choice for the calorie conscious,
but it makes a great cake or dinner party dessert.

Serves 16
Preparation time 15 minutes
Cooking time 25 minutes

**5 ounces gluten-free, dark sweet
  chocolate**
grated rind and juice 1 orange
few drops rum extract (optional)
**10 tablespoons (1¼ sticks) unsalted
  butter, softened**
⅔ cup granulated sugar
4 eggs, separated
1¼ cups ground almonds

for the chocolate frosting
**5 ounces gluten-free, dark sweet
  chocolate**
7 tablespoons unsalted butter

for the topping (optional)
8–16 crystallized violet petals

Nutritional information:
Cal 264 (1102 kJ) Protein 4 g Carb 18 g
Fat 20 g Saturated fat 40 g Fiber 0.5 g

1 Preheat the oven to 350°F. Grease and line two 8-inch cake
pans. Melt together the chocolate, orange rind and juice, and
rum extract, if using, in a heatproof bowl over a saucepan of
simmering water.

2 Place the butter and all but 1 tablespoon of the sugar in a large
bowl and beat together until pale and fluffy. Beat in the egg
yolks, one at a time, then stir in the melted chocolate.

3 Place the egg whites in a large clean bowl; whisk until they form
soft peaks. Add the remaining sugar and whisk until stiff peaks
form. Fold the egg whites into the chocolate mixture with the ground
almonds, then spoon into the prepared cake pans.

4 Place in the preheated oven for 20–25 minutes, until the sides
are cooked but the center is still a little unset. Remove the cakes
from the oven, let cool for a few minutes in the pans, then turn out
gently onto a wire rack.

5 For the frosting, melt the chocolate as before, then whisk in the
butter, a tablespoon at a time, until melted. Remove from the
heat and whisk occasionally until cool. Fill and frost the cooled cakes
with the chocolate mixture. Top with crystallized violet petals if liked.

pear and marzipan loaf

The combination of sticky pear and melting marzipan
is fabulous in this loaf.

Serves 12
Preparation time 10 minutes, plus
soaking overnight
Cooking time 1–1½ hours

1 cup golden raisins
1½ cups dried pears, chopped
2 tablespoons apple juice
few drops almond extract
1 cup plus 2 tablespoons marzipan, cut
into small cubes and frozen
3 tablespoons ground almonds
6 tablespoons granulated sugar
7 tablespoons butter, softened
2 eggs, beaten
1 cup rice flour

Nutritional information:
Cal 344 (1438 kJ) Protein 5 g Carb 52 g
Fat 13 g Saturated fat 5 g Fiber 4 g

1 Place the golden raisins, pears, apple juice, and almond extract in a nonmetallic bowl, cover, and let stand overnight.

2 Preheat the oven to 300°F. Grease and line a 2-pound loaf pan. Place all the remaining ingredients in a large bowl and beat together, stirring in the soaked fruit until well combined.

3 Spoon the mixture into the prepared pan, then place in the preheated oven for 1–1½ hours, until a skewer inserted in the middle comes out clean. Remove the cake from the oven and transfer to a wire rack to cool.

espresso cream gâteau

This gâteau, which is quick and easy to make, is a great choice for an adult birthday cake.

Serves 10
Preparation time 10 minutes
Cooking time 25 minutes

1 cup (2 sticks) butter, softened
1 cup granulated sugar
4 eggs
1½ cups rice flour
2 teaspoons gluten-free baking powder
1 tablespoon instant coffee, dissolved
  in 1 tablespoon boiling water

for the filling and topping
1 cup heavy cream
1 teaspoon instant coffee, dissolved
  in 1 teaspoon boiling water
1 tablespoon confectioners' sugar
handful gluten-free, chocolate-covered
  coffee beans
1 teaspoon cocoa powder

Nutritional information:
Cal 452 (1889 kJ) Protein 6 g Carb 40 g
Fat 30 g Saturated fat 19 g Fiber 1 g

1 Preheat the oven to 400°F. Grease two 8-inch cake pans and dust with rice flour. Place all the cake ingredients in a food processor and whiz until smooth, or beat together in a large bowl.

2 Spoon the mixture into the prepared pans, then place them in the preheated oven for 20–25 minutes, until golden and just firm to the touch. Remove the cakes from the oven and transfer to a wire rack to cool.

3 In a large bowl, whisk the cream, coffee, and confectioners' sugar until the mixture forms soft peaks. Sandwich the cakes together with half of the cream, then smooth the rest over the top. Scatter over the coffee beans and dust with cocoa powder.

lemon drizzle loaf

Citrusy and sweet, this cake is a real afternoon treat.

Serves 12
Preparation time 10 minutes
Cooking time 40 minutes

1 cup (2 sticks) butter, softened
1 cup granulated sugar
1½ cups brown rice flour
2 teaspoons gluten-free baking powder
4 eggs, beaten
grated rind and juice 1 lemon

for the lemon drizzle
grated rind and juice 2 lemons
½ cup granulated sugar

Nutritional information:
Cal 334 (1396 kJ) Protein 5 g Carb 41 g
Fat 18 g Saturated fat 11 g Fiber 1 g

1 Preheat the oven to 350°F. Grease and line a 2-pound loaf pan. Place all the cake ingredients in a food processor and whiz until smooth, or beat together in a large bowl.

2 Pour the mixture into the prepared pan and place in the preheated oven for 35–40 minutes, until golden and firm to the touch. Remove the loaf from the oven and transfer to a wire rack.

3 Prick holes all over the cake with a toothpick. Place the drizzle ingredients in a bowl and mix together, then drizzle the liquid over the warm loaf. Let stand until completely cold. Decorate with a twist of lemon rind if desired.

beet
speckled cake

This moist and beautifully colored cake will make a big impression as an afternoon snack.

Serves 10
Preparation time 15 minutes
Cooking time 50 minutes

14 tablespoons (1¾ sticks) butter, melted
1 cup packed light brown sugar
2–3 medium beets (about 7 ounces), peeled and grated
1¼ cups mixed nuts, toasted and chopped
3 eggs, separated
1 teaspoon gluten-free baking powder
½ teaspoon ground cinnamon
grated rind and juice 1 orange
1¼ cups rice flour
3 tablespoons ground almonds

for the decoration
1 cup cream cheese
1 tablespoon confectioners' sugar
1 cup whole mixed nuts

Nutritional information:
Cal 595 (2487 kJ) **Protein** 12 g **Carb** 38 g
Fat 44 g **Saturated fat** 19 g **Fiber** 4 g

SHOWN ON PAGES 38–39

1 Preheat the oven to 400°F. Grease an 8-inch round, deep cake pan. Place the butter and sugar in a large bowl and whisk together until pale. Stir in the beets, two-thirds of the nuts, and the egg yolks.

2 In another bowl, stir together the baking powder, cinnamon, orange rind and juice, rice flour, and ground almonds. Add to the beet mixture and beat until smooth. In a separate clean bowl, whisk the egg whites until they form soft peaks, then fold them into the beet mixture.

3 Spoon the mixture into the prepared pan and place in the preheated oven for 45–50 minutes. Remove the cake from the oven and transfer to a wire rack to cool.

4 Place the cream cheese and confectioners' sugar in a bowl and beat together, then smooth the frosting over the top of the cake. Decorate with the whole nuts.

banana and date bread

This is a real favorite with both young and old.
Spread with a little butter for an afternoon treat.

Serves 12
Preparation time 20 minutes
Cooking time 1 hour

⅔ cup pitted dates, roughly chopped
1 teaspoon baking soda
2 tablespoons boiling water
7 tablepsoons butter, softened
½ cup granulated sugar
2 eggs, beaten
3 large bananas, mashed
1¼ cups rice flour
⅓ cup cornstarch
1 teaspoon gluten-free baking powder

Nutritional information:
Cal 215 (899 kJ) Protein 4 g Carb 33 g
Fat 8 g Saturated fat 2 g Fiber 2 g

1 Preheat the oven to 350°F. Grease and line a 2-pound loaf pan. Place the dates and baking soda in a small bowl and pour over the water. Set aside for 10 minutes.

2 Meanwhile, place the butter and sugar in a large bowl and beat together until light and fluffy. Stir in the remaining ingredients, including the date mixture, and combine well.

3 Spoon the mixture into the prepared pan and place in the preheated oven for about 1 hour, until nicely browned and firm to the touch. Remove the loaf from the oven and transfer to a wire rack to cool. If you like, you could add a handful of roughly chopped mixed nuts to the mixture.

tropical fruit cake

The tropical fruit mixture provides a good alternative
to a traditional fruitcake and has a lighter flavor.

Serves 14
Preparation time 15 minutes, plus
  soaking overnight
Cooking time 1½–2 hours

grated rind and juice 2 oranges
grated rind 1 lemon
2 cups raisins
3 cups dried tropical fruit, chopped
1 tablespoon crystallized ginger, chopped
3 tablespoons brandy
1 cup (2 sticks) butter, softened
1 cup packed light brown sugar
⅔ cup plus soy flour
¾ cup rice flour
1 teaspoon allspice
¾ cup ground almonds
4 eggs, beaten

To decorate
2 cups dried fruit or nuts
2 tablespoons apricot jam

Nutritional information:
Cal 436 (1822 kJ) **Protein** 7 g **Carb** 65 g
Fat 18 g **Saturated fat** 10 g **Fiber** 3 g

1 Place the orange rind and juice, lemon rind, raisins, dried fruit (we used papaya, peach, cranberries, apricots, and pineapple), ginger, and brandy in a nonmetallic bowl, stir, and cover, then let stand overnight for the fruit to absorb the liquid.

2 Preheat the oven to 325°F. Grease and line a 7-inch square, deep cake pan (or an 8-inch round pan) and tie a double thickness of brown craft paper or newspaper around the outside.

3 Place the butter and sugar in a bowl and beat together until light and fluffy. In another bowl, sift the flours and allspice and stir in the ground almonds. Gradually add the beaten eggs to the creamed butter, adding a little flour mixture if it begins to curdle. Fold in the remaining flour mixture and the soaked fruit and any juice, then spoon into the prepared pn.

4 Place in the preheated oven for 1½–2 hours, or until a skewer inserted in the middle of the cake comes out clean. Remove the cake from the oven and transfer to a wire rack to cool. Decorate with dried fruit or nuts and glaze with apricot jam push through a sieve and warmed.

carrot cake with passion-fruit topping

Moist and flavorsome, you can't beat a piece of carrot cake with a cup of tea or coffee!

Serves 12
Preparation time 10 minutes
Cooking time 40 minutes

2¼ cups rice flour
1 tablespoon gluten-free baking powder
1 teaspoon allspice
1 cup packed light brown sugar
4 medium carrots, peeled and grated
1½ cups walnuts, chopped
½ cup olive oil or rapeseed oil
4 tablespoons crème fraîche or sour cream
3 eggs

for the topping
1 cup cream cheese
2 tablespoons confectioners' sugar
2 passion fruits, flesh removed

Nutritional information:
Cal 467 (1952 kJ) Protein 9 g Carb 43 g
Fat 30 g Saturated fat 8 g Fiber 3 g

1 Preheat the oven to 350°F. Grease and line an 8-inch springform cake pan. Sift the flour, baking powder, and allspice together into a large bowl. Stir in the sugar, carrots, and walnuts.

2 Place the oil, crème fraîche (or sour cream), and eggs in another bowl and beat together, then stir into the dry ingredients. Spoon the mixture into the pan and place in the preheated oven for 35–40 minutes, until a skewer inserted in the middle comes out clean. Remove the cake from the oven and transfer to a wire rack to cool.

3 To make the topping, place the cream cheese, confectioners' sugar and passion-fruit flesh in a bowl and beat together. Smooth over the cake.

pistachio and citrus sand cake

This is a sandy textured cake with a delicious
fresh flavor and aroma.

Serves 14
Preparation time 10 minutes
Cooking time 50 minutes

14 tablespoons (1¾ sticks) butter,
  softened
6 tablespoons granulated sugar
3 eggs, beaten
1¼ cups corn flour
¾ cup ground almonds
1 teaspoon gluten-free baking powder
grated rind 1 orange
⅔ cup unsalted, shelled pistachios,
  roughly chopped

for the syrup topping
½ cup granulated sugar
grated rind and juice 1 lemon
grated rind and juice 1 orange

Nutritional information:
Cal 281 (1175kJ) Protein 4 g Carb 27 g
Fat 18 g Saturated fat 9 g Fiber 1 g

1 Preheat the oven to 350°F. Grease a 9-inch bundt pan and dust lightly with a little corn flour. Place the butter and sugar in a large bowl and beat together. Add a little of the beaten eggs and the corn flour alternately, beating well, then stir in the remaining ingredients.

2 Spoon the mixture into the prepared pan and place in the preheated oven for about 50 minutes, until golden and a skewer inserted in the middle comes out clean. Remove the cake from the oven and transfer to a wire rack to cool.

3 Place the syrup ingredients in a saucepan, warm through until the sugar has dissolved, then boil for 2 minutes. Cool a little, then pour over the cake. Serve in wedges with a little crème fraîche or heavy cream.

hazelnut meringue stack

Light and airy meringue with a chewy center—an unbeatable dessert for a special occasion.

Serves 8
Preparation time 10 minutes
Cooking time 45 minutes, plus cooling

4 egg whites
1 cup granulated sugar
1 teaspoon white wine vinegar
¾ cup hazelnuts, toasted and roughly chopped
1 cup heavy cream
2 cups raspberries
a little cocoa powder for dusting

Nutritional information:
Cal 298 (1246 kJ) Protein 4 g Carb 32 g
Fat 18 g Saturated fat 7 g Fiber 2 g

1 Preheat the oven to 300°F. Line three baking sheets with wax paper. Place the egg whites in a large clean bowl and whisk until they form stiff peaks. Add half the sugar and continue to whisk until thick and glossy, then add the remaining sugar and the vinegar and whisk for 15 seconds.

2 Fold half of the hazelnuts into the mixture, then divide it between the three prepared sheets, spooning the meringue into rounds roughly 7 inches in diameter. Place in the preheated oven for 45 minutes, then switch off the oven and let the meringue cool in the oven.

3 Whisk the cream until it forms soft peaks, spoon the cream over two of the meringues, and top with the raspberries and remaining nuts, keeping back a few raspberries for decoration. Stack the meringues with the plain one on top, then dust with a little cocoa powder and decorate with the remaining raspberries. Eat on the same day or chill for up to 2 days.

blackberry and almond cake

This light sponge cake has a decadent mascarpone cream filling that complements it perfectly.

Serves 10
Preparation time 10 minutes
Cooking time 40 minutes

1½ cups almonds
6 eggs, separated
2 cups confectioners' sugar, sifted
1½ cups gluten-free, fresh bread crumbs
6 tablespoons butter, melted
2 cups blackberries, roughly crushed

for the filling
1 cup mascarpone cheese
2 tablespoons confectioners' sugar
few drops vanilla extract

Nutritional information:
Cal 371 (1551 kJ) **Protein** 7 g **Carb** 22 g
Fat 28 g **Saturated fat** 13 g **Fiber** 3 g

1 Preheat the oven to 350°F. Grease and line a 9-inch, deep springform pan. Place the almonds on a baking sheet and place in the preheated oven for 10 minutes, until golden. Let cool a little, then place in a food processor or liquidizer and whiz until they resemble fine bread crumbs.

2 Place the egg whites in a large clean bowl and whisk until they form soft peaks. Add 2 tablespoons of the confectioners' sugar and whisk until firm. Place the egg yolks in a separate bowl with the remaining confectioners' sugar and whisk until pale. Fold in the bread crumbs, butter, half the blackberries, and the egg whites, then transfer to the prepared pan. Place in the oven for 40 minutes, then transfer to a wire rack to cool.

3 Place the filling ingredients in a bowl and beat together, along with the the remaining blackberries. Slice the cake in half and fill with the mascarpone mixture.

cherry and ricotta cake

Adding ricotta cheese keeps this cake lovely and moist, and the flavors and textures blend beautifully.

Serves 12
Preparation time 10 minutes
Cooking time 1½ hours

1¼ cups polenta
1¼ cups brown rice flour
1 teaspoon gluten-free baking powder
few drops almond extract
1 cup granulated sugar
1 cup ricotta cheese
7 tablespoons butter, melted
10-ounce can black cherries, in their
   juice

for the topping:
2 tablespoons light brown sugar
⅓ cup blanched almonds, cut into
   slivers

Nutritional information:
Cal 393 (1643 kJ) **Protein** 6 g **Carb** 58 g
Fat 16 g **Saturated fat** 9 g **Fiber** 3 g

1 Preheat the oven to 325°F. Grease and lightly flour an 8-inch springform cake pan. Sift the polenta, flour, and baking powder together into a large bowl, then beat in the almond extract, sugar, ricotta cheese, butter, and cherries with their juice.

2 Spoon the mixture into the prepared pan, mix together the topping ingredients and sprinkle over the top of the cake. Place the cake in the preheated oven for 1½ hours, until golden and a skewer inserted in the middle comes out clean. Remove the cake from the oven and transfer to a wire rack to cool.

tempting sheet bakes and cookies

coconut macaroons

Light but with a chewy texture, these classic macaroons make a tempting afternoon nibble.

Makes 14 macaroons
Preparation time 10 minutes
Cooking time 20 minutes

3 egg whites
⅔ cup granulated sugar
2 tablespoons ground almonds
2¾ cups shredded coconut

Nutritional information:
Cal 165 (690 kJ) **Protein** 2 g **Carb** 12 g
Fat 12 g **Saturated fat** 9 g **Fiber** 3 g

1 Preheat the oven to 350°F. Line two baking sheets with wax paper, or use edible rice paper. Place the egg whites in a large clean bowl and whisk until they form stiff peaks. Gradually whisk in the sugar until thick and glossy, then fold in the almonds and coconut.

2 Place seven spoonfuls of the mixture on each tray and place in the preheated oven for 15–20 minutes, until turning golden. Remove from the oven and transfer to a wire rack to cool.

lemon madeleines

These light lemony bites make a delicate addition
to an afternoon snack.

Makes 36 cakes
Preparation time 10 minutes, plus
  resting time of 30 minutes
Cooking time 8 minutes

2 large eggs
4 tablespoons granulated sugar
⅔ cup white rice flour
7 tablespoons butter, melted, plus extra
  for greasing
grated rind 1 lemon
confectioners' sugar to dust

Nutritional information:
Cal 44 (184 kJ) Protein 1 g Carb 4 g
Fat 2 g Saturated fat 1 g Fiber 0 g

1 Place the eggs and sugar in a large bowl and whisk together until pale and thick. Sift the flour into the mixture and fold it in. Drizzle in the melted butter, add the lemon rind, and stir to combine. Set the mixture aside for half an hour.

2 Preheat the oven to 425°F. Generously grease 36 holes in three 12-hole madeleine or mini muffin pans with plenty of butter. Spoon about 1 teaspoon of mixture into each mold and place in the preheated oven for about 8 minutes, until just firm.

3 Remove the madeleines from the oven and transfer to a wire rack to cool, then dust generously with confectioners' sugar. They are best eaten on the same day.

chocolate caramel shortbread

A real favorite: creamy caramel on light, crisp shortbread topped with thick swirls of chocolate.

Makes 15 pieces
Preparation time 20 minutes, plus chilling
Cooking time 15 minutes

7 tablespoons butter, softened
¼ cup granulated sugar
⅔ cup brown rice flour
¾ cup corn flour

for the caramel
7 tablespoons butter
¼ cup packed light brown sugar
13-ounce can condensed milk

for the topping
3½ ounces gluten-free white chocolate
3½ ounces gluten-free dark sweet chocolate

Nutritional information:
Cal 328 (1371 kJ) Protein 4 g Carb 40 g
Fat 17 g Saturated fat 11 g Fiber 0 g

1 Preheat the oven to 400°F. Place the butter and sugar in a large bowl and beat together until light and fluffy, then stir in the flours until well combined. Press the shortbread into an 11 x 7-inch baking pan, then place in the preheated oven for 10–12 minutes, until golden.

2 Meanwhile, place the caramel ingredients in a heavy-based saucepan and heat over a low heat until the sugar has dissolved, then cook for 5 minutes, stirring continuously. Remove from the heat and let cool a little, then pour the caramel over the shortbread base and let cool.

3 Place the white and dark chocolates in separate heatproof bowls over saucepans of simmering water and melt. When the caramel is firm, spoon alternate spoonfuls of the white and dark chocolates over the caramel, tap the pan on the work surface so that the different chocolates join, then use a knife to make swirls in the chocolate. Refrigerate until set, then cut into 15 squares.

fruity shortbread fingers

Full of flavor and texture, these are a hit with children and make a filling yet healthy addition to lunch boxes.

Makes 12 bars
Preparation time 10 minutes
Cooking time 25 minutes

7 tablespoons butter, softened
¼ cup granulated sugar
⅔ cup brown rice flour
¾ cup corn flour
1 cup dried dates, roughly chopped
grated rind and juice 1 orange

for the topping
¼ cup clear honey
4 tablespoons butter, melted
1½ cups gluten-free cornflakes, roughly crushed
2 tablespoons shredded coconut
½ cup dried apricots, chopped
2 tablespoons mixed seeds, such as pumpkin and sunflower

Nutritional information:
Cal 272 (1137 kJ) Protein 2 g Carb 40 g
Fat 13 g Saturated fat 8 g Fiber 0 g

1 Preheat the oven to 400°F. Place the butter and sugar in a large bowl and beat together until light and fluffy, then stir in the flours until well combined. Press the shortbread into an 11 x 7-inch baking pan and place in the preheated oven for 10 minutes.

2 Meanwhile, place the dates and orange rind and juice in a small saucepan, bring to a boil, and simmer gently until pulpy. Remove from the heat and let cool a little, then spread the mixture over the shortbread base.

3 Place all the topping ingredients in a bowl and mix together, spoon the mixture over the dates, and press down gently. Place in the oven for 12–15 minutes, until golden. Remove from the oven, let cool a little, then cut into 12 bars and let cool completely before removing them from the pan.

espresso and white chocolate brownies

These squidgy white chocolate brownies are given a twist with the addition of some espresso.

Makes 15 brownies
Preparation time 10 minutes
Cooking time 30 minutes

3 ounces gluten-free white chocolate
6 tablespoons butter
¾ cup packed light brown sugar
2 eggs, beaten
few drops vanilla extract
½ cup ground almonds
⅔ cup rice flour
2 teaspoons instant espresso coffee,
   dissolved in 1 tablespoon water
¾ cup walnuts, toasted and roughly
   chopped

Nutritional information:
Cal 210 (878 kJ) Protein 3 g Carb 22 g
Fat 13 g Saturated fat 2 g Fiber 0 g

1 Preheat the oven to 350°F. Grease and line an 11 x 7-inch baking pan. Place the chocolate and butter in a large heatproof bowl over a pan of simmering water and melt. Stir all the remaining ingredients in roughly, then pour into the prepared pan.

2 Place in the preheated oven for 30 minutes, until slightly springy in the center. Remove from the oven and let cool for 10 minutes before dividing into 15 squares, then cool on a wire rack.

chewy nutty chocolate brownies

These spectacular gooey squares are great for a treat with coffee or served as a dessert with a little cream or gluten-free ice cream.

Makes 15 pieces
Preparation time 10 minutes
Cooking time 30 minutes

3 ounces gluten-free dark sweet chocolate
7 tablespoons butter
1 cup packed light brown sugar
2 eggs, beaten
few drops vanilla extract
½ cup ground almonds
2 tablespoons plus 1½ teaspoons brown rice flour
1 cup mixed nuts, toasted and roughly chopped

Nutritional information:
Cal 230 (961 kJ) Protein 3 g Carb 19 g
Fat 16 g Saturated fat 5 g Fiber 1 g

1 Preheat the oven to 350°F. Grease and line an 11 x 7-inch baking pan. Place the chocolate and butter in a large heatproof bowl over a pan of simmering water and melt. Stir in all the remaining ingredients and combine well.

2 Pour the mixture into the prepared pan and place in the preheated oven for 30 minutes, until slightly springy in the center. Remove from the oven and cool for 10 minutes in the pan, then mark to divide into 15 squares.

hazelnut and chocolate macaroons

These flavorsome macaroons are different from the traditional coconut version, but no less delicious.

Makes 12 macaroons
Preparation time 10 minutes
Cooking time 20 minutes

3 egg whites
⅔ cup granulated sugar
1 cup hazelnuts, toasted and ground
2 tablespoons cocoa powder
few drops vanilla extract
3½ ounces gluten-free milk chocolate

Nutritional information:
Cal 148 (619 kJ) Protein 4 g Carb 11 g
Fat 10 g Saturated fat 1 g Fiber 2 g

1 Preheat the oven to 350°F. Line two baking sheets with wax paper, or you could use edible rice paper. Place the egg whites in a large clean bowl and whisk until they form stiff peaks. Gradually whisk in the sugar until thick and glossy, then fold in the hazelnuts, cocoa powder, and vanilla extract.

2 Place six spoonfuls of mixture on each sheet and place in the preheated oven for 15–20 minutes. Remove from the oven and transfer to a wire rack to cool.

3 Place the chocolate in a heatproof bowl over a pan of simmering water and melt, then drizzle it over the macaroons.

plum pastries

These are good as a dessert for summer entertaining when plums are juicy and ripe.

Makes 6 pastries
Preparation time 15 minutes, plus chilling
Cooking time 25 minutes

½ cup brown rice flour
½ cup polenta
½ teaspoon xanthan gum
pinch of allspice
grated rind ½ lemon
7 tablespoons butter, cubed
1 tablespoon granulated sugar
1 egg yolk, beaten
½ cup marzipan, grated
3 tablespoons crème fraîche or heavy cream
6 medium plums (about 1 pound), halved and pitted
2 tablespoons apricot jam, warmed

Nutritional information:
Cal 247 (1032 kJ) Protein 3 g Carb 38 g
Fat 10 g Saturated fat 5 g Fiber 1 g

1 Place the flour, polenta, xanthan gum, allspice, lemon rind, butter, and sugar in a food processor and whiz until the mixture resembles fine bread crumbs, or rub in by hand in a large bowl.

2 Gently add the egg yolk and mix in, using a knife, adding a little cold water if the mixture is too dry. Knead the mixture into a ball, wrap closely and chill for 30 minutes.

3 Preheat the oven to 400°F. Divide the pastry into six, then roll each piece out on a surface dusted lightly with rice flour to a rectangle approximately 4 x 2½ inches. Mark a border about ½ inch from the edge of the pastry.

4 Place the pastry on a baking sheet. Mix together the marzipan and crème fraîche and spoon over the pastry within the border; arrange the plums over the marzipan mixture and place in the preheated oven for 20–25 minutes, until the pastry is golden and the plums begin to ooze a little juice. Remove the pastries from the oven and let cool. Brush each with a little jam. Delicious served with cream or crème fraîche for dessert.

bakewell slice

This gluten-free version of a traditional British cake
tastes just as good as the original.

Makes 12 pieces
Preparation time 20 minutes
Cooking time 25 minutes

½ cup polenta
½ cup brown rice flour
½ teaspoon xanthan gum
grated rind 1 lemon
7 tablespoons butter, cubed
1 tablespoon granulated sugar
1 egg yolk, beaten
4 tablespoons raspberry jam

for the sponge
2 eggs
½ cup granulated sugar
¾ cup rice flour
8 tablespoons (1 stick) butter
½ cup ground almonds
1 teaspoon gluten-free baking powder
⅓ cup flaked almonds

Nutritional information:
Cal 301 (1258 kJ) Protein 5 g Carb 30 g
Fat 18 g Saturated fat 9 g Fiber 1 g

1 Preheat the oven to 400°F. Place the polenta, flour, xanthan gum, lemon rind, butter, and sugar in a food processor and whiz until the mixture resembles fine bread crumbs, or rub in by hand in a large bowl. Add the egg yolk and gently mix in, using a knife, adding a little cold water if the mixture is too dry.

2 Place the pastry in an 11 x 7-inch, deep baking pan and press it out to line the pan. Spread the jam over it.

3 Place all the sponge ingredients except the flaked almonds in a food processor and whiz until smooth, or beat in a large bowl. Spoon the mixture into the baking pan, and place in the preheated oven for 20–25 minutes, until just firm and risen. Remove the tart from the oven and let cool. Toast the flaked almonds for a few minutes under a broiler until brown and scatter them over the top. Cut into 12 pieces.

pistachio and choc chip shortbread

This light, melt-in-the-mouth shortbread has the ever-popular flavor of chocolate in it as well as the more unusual addition of pistachios.

Makes 12 pieces
Preparation time 10 minutes
Cooking time 20 minutes

7 tablespoons butter, softened
¼ cup superfine sugar
⅔ cup rice flour
¾ cup corn flour
2 ounces gluten-free dark sweet chocolate drops or gluten-free dark sweet chocolate, chopped
⅓ cup pistachios, chopped

for the decoration
3 ounces gluten-free dark sweet chocolate, melted

Nutritional information:
Cal 175 (732 kJ) **Protein** 1 g **Carb** 22 g
Fat 10 g **Saturated fat** 2 g **Fiber** 0 g

SHOWN ON PAGES 66–67

1 Preheat the oven to 350°F. Place the butter and sugar in a large bowl and beat together until light and fluffy. Stir in the remaining ingredients until well combined. Press the mixture into an 11 x 7-inch baking pan and place in the preheated oven for 20 minutes until golden.

2 Remove the shortbread from the oven, mark to divide into 12 triangles, then place on a wire rack to cool completely before removing from the pan. It is sometimes easier to remove the shortbread from the pan once it has been chilled a little. Drizzle with the melted chocolate.

peanutty squares

These are simple to make but should be served in small pieces, as the combination of peanut butter and chocolate makes them rich.

Makes 24 pieces
Preparation time 10 minutes
Cooking time 25 minutes

4 tablespoons butter, softened
1 cup confectioners' sugar
⅔ cup gluten-free, crunchy peanut butter
⅔ cup brown rice flour
1 egg, beaten
7 ounces gluten-free, dark sweet chocolate
1 tablespoon butter

Nutritional information:
Cal 156 (652 kJ) Protein 3 g Carb 17 g
Fat 9 g Saturated fat 4 g Fiber 1 g

1 Preheat the oven to 400°F. Grease and line a 9-inch square baking pan. Place the butter and sugar in a large bowl, beat together until pale and fluffy, then stir in the peanut butter, flour, and egg.

2 Spoon the mixture into the prepared pan and place in the preheated oven for 20–25 minutes. Remove the pan from the oven and let cool.

3 Place the chocolate and butter in a heatproof bowl over a pan of simmering water and let the chocolate melt, then pour over the baked peanut mixture. Let cool until the chocolate is set, then mark to divide into 24 small squares.

lemon, pistachio, and fruit squares

Chewy and with so many great flavors, these are great for a high-energy snack.

Makes 15–20 pieces
Preparation time 10 minutes
Cooking time 20 minutes

grated rind 1 lemon
6 tablespoons dried dates, chopped
½ cup unsalted pistachios, chopped
¾ cup flaked almonds, chopped
½ cup packed light brown sugar
1¼ cups millet flakes
1½ cups gluten-free cornflakes, lightly crushed
13-ounce can condensed milk
3 tablespoons mixed seeds, such as pumpkin and sunflower

Nutritional information:
Cal 174 (728 kJ) Protein 4 g Carb 26 g
Fat 6 g Saturated fat 2 g Fiber 2 g

1 Preheat the oven to 350°F. Place all the ingredients in a large bowl and mix together. Spoon into an 11 x 7-inch baking pan and place in the preheated oven for 20 minutes.

2 Remove from the oven, let cool, then mark to divide into 15–20 squares and chill until firm. If you fancy, you could drizzle the top with some melted chocolate once the squares are cooled.

lemony poppets

These lemon and ground almond creations are so
light, one won't be enough!

Makes 30 poppets
Preparation time 10 minutes, plus
  chilling
Cooking time 20 minutes

½ cup vegetable shortening
½ cup butter, softened
½ cup granulated sugar
1 egg yolk
grated rind 1 lemon
1 tablespoon milk
1¼ cups brown rice flour
2 tablespoons corn flour
½ cup ground almonds

Nutritional information:
Cal 98 (410 kJ) Protein 0 g Carb 10 g
Fat 6 g Saturated fat 4 g Fiber 0 g

1 Line two baking sheets with wax paper. Place all the ingredients in a food processor and whiz until smooth, or beat together in a large bowl until light and smooth.

2 Spoon the mixture onto a surface dusted lightly with rice flour, divide it into 30, and roll into balls. Place on the prepared baking sheets, flatten slightly with your thumb and chill for 30 minutes.

3 Meanwhile, preheat the oven to 350°F. Place in the preheated oven for about 20 minutes, until golden. Remove from the oven and let cool on the baking sheets.

walnut cookies

These are easy to make, and you can use other flavors,
such as raisins or chocolate chips, to suit your taste.

Makes 30 cookies
Preparation time 10 minutes
Cooking time 20 minutes

8 tablespoons (1 stick) butter, softened
½ cup granulated sugar
1 egg yolk
¾ cup rice flour
1 teaspoon gluten-free baking powder
¾ cup walnuts, chopped

Nutritional information:
Cal 86 (359 kJ) Protein 1 g Carb 8 g
Fat 6 g Saturated fat 2 g Fiber 0 g

1 Preheat the oven to 350°F. Place the butter and sugar in a large bowl and beat together until light and fluffy. Beat in the egg yolk, followed by the remaining ingredients to create a smooth soft dough.

2 Place walnut-sized pieces of the mixture onto baking sheets and place in the preheated oven for 15–20 minutes, until golden. Remove the cookies from the oven, let stand for a few minutes to harden, then transfer to a wire rack to cool.

chocolate chip cookies

This gluten-free version of these perennial favorites is light, crunchy, and simply irresistible.

Makes 30 cookies
Preparation time 10 minutes
Cooking time 10 minutes

6 tablespoons butter, softened
7 tablespoons granulated sugar
6 tablespoons light brown sugar
1 egg, beaten
¾ cup brown rice flour
½ teaspoon baking soda
1 tablespoon cocoa powder
3 ounces gluten-free dark, sweet
   chocolate chips

Nutritional information:
Cal 75 (314 kJ) Protein 0 g Carb 12 g
Fat 3 g Saturated fat 2 g Fiber 0 g

1 Preheat the oven to 350°F. Place all the ingredients except the chocolate chips in a food processor and whiz until smooth, or beat together in a large bowl. Stir in the chocolate chips, and bring the mixture together with your hands to form a ball.

2 On a surface dusted lightly with rice flour, divide the mixture into 30 balls, then place them on baking sheets, well spaced apart, pressing down gently with the back of a fork.

3 Place in the preheated oven for 8–10 minutes. Remove the cookies from the oven, let stand for a few minutes to harden, then transfer to a wire rack to cool.

apricot almond crunch cookies

These little chewy morsels are great
for an afternoon treat.

Makes 15 cookies
Preparation time 10 minutes
Cooking time 15 minutes

7 tablespoons butter
¼ cup packed light brown sugar
1 tablespoon light corn syrup
⅔ cup brown rice flour
½ teaspoon gluten-free baking powder
2½ cups millet flakes
½ cup dried apricots, chopped
½ cup blanched almonds, toasted and
  roughly chopped

Nutritional information:
Cal 137 (573 kJ) Protein 2 g Carb 15 g
Fat 8 g Saturated fat 6 g Fiber 1 g

1 Preheat the oven to 350°F. Place the butter, sugar, and syrup in a large saucepan over a gentle heat and melt together. Stir in the remaining ingredients so that everything is well mixed.

2 Scrape the mixture out onto a surface lightly dusted with rice flour and use your hands to bring it together. Divide the mixture into 15 pieces, roll into balls, then place on two baking sheets and flatten to rounds about 2 inches in diameter.

3 Place in the preheated oven for 15 minutes. Remove the cookies from the oven, let stand for a few minutes to harden, then transfer to a wire rack to cool.

crisp ginger cookies

Not only deliciously crisp but also perfect for dunking in tea or coffee.

Makes 20 cookies
Preparation time 10 minutes
Cooking time 15 minutes

1¼ **cups brown rice flour**
½ **cup ground almonds**
½ **teaspoon ground ginger**
½ **cup granulated sugar**
1 piece preserved ginger, finely chopped
1 egg, beaten
7 tablespoons butter, melted

Nutritional information:
Cal 111 (464 kJ) Protein 1 g Carb 15 g
Fat 6 g Saturated fat 3 g Fiber 0 g

1 Preheat the oven to 350°F. Place all the dry ingredients and the preserved ginger in a large bowl and stir together. Combine the egg and butter and stir into the flour mixture.

2 Scrape the mixture out onto a surface lightly dusted with rice flour and use your hands to bring it together. Divide the mixture into 20 pieces, roll into balls then place on two–three baking sheets, pressing down slightly.

3 Place in the preheated oven for 12–15 minutes, until golden. Remove the cookies from the oven, let stand for a few minutes to harden, then transfer to a wire rack to cool.

orange and polenta crispy cookies

Polenta gives these cookies a really crisp and crunchy texture.

Makes 20 cookies
Preparation time 10 minutes, plus chilling
Cooking time 8 minutes

½ cup polenta
2 tablespoons plus 1½ teaspoons rice flour
¼ cup ground almonds
½ teaspoon gluten-free baking powder
⅔ cup confectioners' sugar
4 tablespoons butter, cubed
1 egg yolk, beaten
grated rind 1 orange
3 tablespoons flaked almonds

Nutritional information:
Cal 67 (280 kJ) Protein 1 g Carb 7 g
Fat 4 g Saturated fat 1 g Fiber 1 g

1 Cover two baking sheets with wax paper. Place the polenta, flour, ground almonds, baking powder, confectioners' sugar, and butter in a food processor and whiz until the mixture resembles fine bread crumbs, or rub in by hand in a large bowl.

2 Stir in the egg yolk and orange rind and bring together to make a dough. Wrap closely and chill for 30 minutes.

3 Preheat the oven to 350°F. Remove the dough from the refrigerator and roll out thinly on a surface dusted lightly with rice flour. Cut into 20 rounds with a 1½-inch cutter. Transfer to the prepared baking sheets, sprinkle with the almonds, and place in the preheated oven for about 8 minutes, until golden. Remove the cookies from the oven, let stand for a few minutes to harden, then transfer to a wire rack to cool.

breads and
biscuits

white loaf

Use on the day of baking for bread or toast that
doesn't turn to crumbs!

Serves 12
Preparation time 20 minutes, plus
rising time
Cooking time 1 hour

4 cups brown rice flour, plus
   a little extra for dusting
1 tablespoon xanthan gum
2 tablespoons skimmed dried milk
   powder
½ teaspoon salt
2 x ¼-ounce package active dried yeast
2 teaspoons granulated sugar
2 cups warm water
2 eggs, beaten
2 tablespoons olive oil

Nutritional information:
Cal 208 (869 kJ) Protein 8 g Carb 40 g
Fat 4 g Saturated fat 0 g Fiber 2 g

SHOWN ON PAGES 92–93

1 Place the flour, xanthan gum, skimmed milk powder, and salt in a large bowl and mix together. Place the yeast, suga,r and water in another bowl and let stand in a warm place for 10 minutes, until frothy. Pour the yeast mixture, eggs, and oil into the dry ingredients and stir together to form a soft dough. Tip the dough out onto a surface dusted lightly with rice flour and knead for 5 minutes.

2 Place the dough in a lightly oiled bowl, cover with a damp kitchen towel or plastic wrap, and let rise in a warm place for about 1 hour, or until doubled in size. Tip the dough out and reknead, then form into a long, oval shape, place on a baking sheet, and let rise again until it has doubled in size.

3 Meanwhile, preheat the oven to 400°F. Score along the top of the loaf a few times using a knife. Place in the preheated oven for 45–50 minutes, or until golden and hollow-sounding when tapped. Remove the loaf from the sheet and return to the oven for 5–10 minutes to crisp it all over. Remove the loaf from the oven and transfer to a wire rack to cool.

soda bread

This great free-form bread is super-quick and
easy to make.

Makes 8 pieces
Preparation time 10 minutes
Cooking time 35 minutes

1¼ cups brown rice flour, plus extra for
　dusting
1¼ cups corn flour
¼ cup rice bran
2 tablespoons skimmed dried milk
　powder
½ teaspoon baking soda
1 teaspoon gluten-free baking powder
good pinch salt
1 teaspoon xanthan gum
pinch of granulated sugar
1 egg, lightly beaten
1¼ cups buttermilk
4 tablespoons water

Nutritional information:
Cal 175 (732 kJ) Protein 8 g Carb 32 g
Fat 2 g Saturated fat 0 g Fiber 4 g

1 Preheat the oven to its highest setting. Place all the dry
ingredients in a large bowl and mix together. Place the egg,
buttermilk, and water in another bowl, mix together, then stir into
the dry ingredients.

2 Tip the mixture out onto a surface dusted lightly with rice flour
and form into a round about 8 inches in diameter. Make marks
to divide into eight segments, then place on a baking sheet and
sprinkle over a little extra rice flour.

3 Place in the preheated oven and cook for 10 minutes, then
reduce the heat to 400°F and continue to cook for about 25
minutes, until golden and hollow-sounding when tapped. Remove the
loaf from the oven and transfer to a wire rack to cool.

feta and herb loaf

This cheesy herb loaf makes a really nice change from the usual gluten-free bread.

Serves 14
Preparation time 10 minutes, plus rising time
Cooking time 45 minutes

1¼ cups polenta
⅔ cup rice flour
¾ cup instant dry milk
pinch salt
¼-ounce package active dried yeast
2 teaspoons granulated sugar
2 teaspoons xanthan gum
3 eggs, beaten
2 tablespoons chopped fresh mixed herbs
2 cups tepid water
⅔ cup feta cheese, crumbled

Nutritional information:
Cal 118 (493 kJ) Protein 6 g Carb 16 g
Fat 3 g Saturated fat 1 g Fiber 1 g

1 Grease and line a 2-pound loaf pan. Sift the polenta, flour, instant milk, and salt into a large bowl and stir well to combine. Stir in the yeast, sugar, and xanthan gum.

2 Place the eggs, herbs, and water in a bowl and mix together. Stir this mixture into the dry ingredients and combine to form a soft dough. Beat for 5 minutes, then stir in the feta cheese. Spoon the mixture into the prepared pan, cover with a clean damp kitchen towel, and let stand in a warm place to rise for about 30 minutes, until the mixture is near the top of the pan.

3 Meanwhile, preheat the oven to 350°F. Place the loaf in the preheated oven for about 45 minutes, until brown and hollow when tapped. Remove the loaf from the oven and transfer to a wire rack to cool.

pumpkin loaf

This simple loaf is delicious served with cheese and chutney, replacing the traditional sandwich for lunch.

Serves 12
Preparation time 10 minutes
Cooking time 1 hour

1½ cups brown rice flour
1½ cups corn flour
pinch salt
½ teaspoon ground cinnamon
½ teaspoon grated nutmeg
2 teaspoons gluten-free baking powder
1 tablespoon xanthan gum
1⅓ cups (10 ounces) cooked pumpkin, pureed
1 tablespoon clear honey
2 tablespoons olive oil
3 eggs, beaten
⅔ cup water

Nutritional information:
Cal 186 (778 kJ) Protein 6 g Carb 30 g
Fat 4 g Saturated fat 0 g Fiber 3 g

1 Preheat the oven to 350°F. grease and line a 2-pound loaf pan. Place all the dry ingredients in a large bowl and mix together. Place the remaining ingredients in another bowl, mix together, then stir into the dry ingredients and beat well.

2 Pour into the prepared pan and place in the preheated oven for about 1 hour, until golden, risen, and firm to the touch. Remove the loaf from the oven and transfer to a wire rack to cool, then serve buttered.

corn bread

An American favorite, this is great served with
soups and casseroles to mop up all the flavors.

Makes 9 pieces
Preparation time 10 minutes
Cooking time 20 minutes

1½ cups polenta
1¼ cups garbanzo flour
2 teaspoons granulated sugar
2 teaspoons gluten-free baking powder
pinch salt
3 scallions, finely sliced
2 tablespoons olive oil
2½ cups milk
1 egg

Nutritional information:
Cal 104 (435 kJ) Protein 5 g Carb 10 g
Fat 4 g Saturated fat 1g Fiber 2 g

1 Preheat the oven to 400°F. Grease an 8-inch square, nonstick baking pan. Place the polenta, flour, sugar, baking powder, salt, and scallions in a large bowl and mix together.

2 In a separate bowl, beat together the oil, milk, and egg, then pour this mixture over the dry ingredients and stir well to combine. Transfer the dough to the prepared pan and place in the preheated oven for 20 minutes, until golden and firm. Cut into nine pieces and let cool.

nutty seed loaf

The nuts and seeds give this loaf a really nice texture as well as plenty of flavor. It's great served toasted.

Makes 8 pieces
Preparation time 10 minutes
Cooking time 25 minutes

2½ cups brown rice flour, plus extra for
   dusting
¼ cup rice bran
2 tablespoons instant dry skimmed milk
½ teaspoon baking soda
1 teaspoon gluten-free baking powder
½–1 teaspoon salt
1 teaspoon xanthan gum
pinch of granulated sugar
⅓ cup mixed seeds, such as sunflower
   and pumpkin
⅓ cup hazelnuts, toasted and roughly
   chopped
1 egg, lightly beaten
1¼ cups buttermilk

Nutritional information:
Cal 263 (1099 kJ) Protein 10 g Carb 37 g
Fat 8 g Saturated fat 1 g Fiber 4 g

1 Preheat the oven to the highest setting. Place all the dry ingredients, including the nuts, in a large bowl and mix together. In a separate bowl, mix together the egg and buttermilk, then stir into the dry ingredients.

2 Tip the dough out onto a surface dusted lightly with rice flour and form into a round about 8 inches in diameter. Mark to divide into eight segments, then place on a baking sheet and dust with a little extra rice flour.

3 Place in the preheated oven for 10 minutes, then reduce the heat to 400°F and continue to cook for about 15 minutes, until the loaf is golden and sounds hollow when tapped. Remove the loaf from the oven and transfer to a wire rack to cool.

walnut loaf

Buckwheat gives this delicious bread an "earthy"
nutty taste with a wonderful aroma.

Serves 12
Preparation time 25 minutes, plus
   rising time
Cooking time 1 hour

2 cups buckwheat flour
3 cups brown rice flour, plus a little
   extra for dusting
1 tablespoon xanthan gum
2 tablespoons instant dry skimmed
   milk
1⅔ cups walnut pieces
½ teaspoon salt
2 x ¼-ounce packages active dried yeast
2 teaspoons granulated sugar
2 cups warm water
2 eggs, beaten
2 tablespoons clear honey
2 tablespoons olive oil

Nutritional information:
Cal 360 (1505 kJ) Protein 8 g Carb 46 g
Fat 16 g Saturated fat 1 g Fiber 1 g

1 Grease a 2-pound loaf pan. Place the flours, xanthan gum, instant milk, walnut pieces, and salt in a large bowl. Place the yeast, sugar, and water in another bowl and let stand in a warm place for 10 minutes, until frothy. Pour the yeast mixture, eggs, honey, and oil into the flour mixture and stir together to form a soft dough. Tip the dough out onto a surface dusted lightly with rice flour and knead for 5 minutes.

2 Place the dough in a lightly oiled bowl, cover with a damp cloth or plastic wrap, and let rise in a warm place for about 1 hour, or until doubled in size. Tip the dough out and reknead, then place in the prepared loaf pan and let rise again.

3 Meanwhile, preheat the oven to 400°F. Place the loaf in the preheated oven for 45–50 minutes, or until golden and hollow-sounding when tapped. Remove the loaf from the pan and return to the oven for 5–10 minutes to crisp it all over. Remove the loaf from the oven and transfer to a wire rack to cool.

buckwheat bread

This is fantastic served warm with butter and jam
for an afternoon snack.

Serves 8
Preparation time 10 minutes, plus
  rising time
Cooking time 50 minutes

1⅔ **cups buckwheat flour**
1¼ **cups brown rice flour**
2 **teaspoons xanthan gum**
2 **tablespoons instant dry milk**
¼-**ounce package active dried yeast**
2 **teaspoons granulated sugar**
1¼ **cups warm water**
2 **eggs, beaten**

for the glaze
1 **egg, beaten**
1 **tablespoon milk**

Nutritional information:
Cal 220 (920 kJ) **Protein** 7 g **Carb** 43 g
Fat 3 g **Saturated fat** 1 g **Fiber** 4 g

1 Place the flours, xanthan gum, and instant milk in a large bowl and mix together. Place the yeast, sugar, and water in another bowl and let stand in a warm place for 15 minutes, until frothy. Pour the yeast mixture into the dry ingredients with the beaten eggs, and bring together to form a soft dough.

2 Tip the dough out onto a surface dusted lightly with rice flour and knead for 5 minutes. Shape the dough into a loaf, place on a baking sheet, and cover with a damp cloth. Let rise for 40 minutes.

3 Preheat the oven to 400°F. Place the egg and milk for the glaze in a bowl, mix together, then brush over the loaf. Place the loaf in the preheated oven for 45–50 minutes, until golden and hollow-sounding when tapped. Remove the loaf from the oven and transfer to a wire rack to cool.

parmesan, olive, and sun-dried tomato loaf

There is a taste of the Mediterranean in this simple loaf.

Serves 14
Preparation time 10 minutes, plus rising time
Cooking time 45 minutes

1¼ cups polenta
⅔ cup rice flour
¾ cup instant dry milk
pinch of salt
¼-ounce package active dried yeast
2 teaspoons granulated sugar
2 teaspoons xanthan gum
3 eggs, beaten
2 tablespoons sun-dried tomato puree
2 cups tepid water
½ cup Parmesan cheese, grated
⅓ cup pitted olives, chopped
2 teaspoons chopped fresh oregano

Nutritional information:
Cal 120 (502 kJ) Protein 6 g Carb 16 g
Fat 3 g Saturated fat 1 g Fiber 2 g

1 Grease and line a 2-pound loaf pan. Sift the polenta, flour, and instant milk together into a large bowl, and stir well to combine. Stir in the yeast, sugar, and xanthan gum.

2 Place the eggs, sun-dried tomato puree, and water in another bowl and mix together, then stir into the dry ingredients and combine to form a soft dough. Beat for 5 minutes, then stir in the remaining ingredients. Spoon the mixture into the prepared pan, cover with a clean damp kitchen towel and let stand in a warm place to rise for about 30 minutes, until the mixture is near the top of the pan.

3 Meanwhile, preheat the oven to 350°F. Place the loaf in the preheated oven for about 45 minutes, until brown and hollow when tapped. Remove the loaf from the oven and transfer to a wire rack to cool.

potato flat bread

A dense bread, this is best served warm from the oven spread with butter.

Serves 12
Preparation time 15 minutes
Cooking time 35 minutes

1 medium potato, chopped into ¾-inch cubes and cooked in boiling water for 10 minutes
1¼ cups milk, warmed
2 eggs, beaten
2⅓ cups brown rice flour
1 teaspoon xanthan gum
2 tablespoons olive oil
1 tablespoon gluten-free baking powder
pinch of salt
2 teaspoons granulated sugar

Nutritional information:
Cal 65 (272 kJ) Protein 2 g Carb 11 g
Fat 1 g Saturated fat 0 g Fiber 1 g

1 Preheat the oven to 400°F. Grease a 9-inch square baking pan. Place the potato, milk, and egg in a large bowl and beat together, then fold in the remaining ingredients.

2 Spoon the mixture into the prepared pan and place in the preheated oven for 30–35 minutes, until golden and firm to the touch. Remove from the oven and let cool in the pan.

olive and sun-dried tomato biscuits

These can be prepared in no time, so you can eat them the same day while still warm from the oven.

Makes 8 biscuits
Preparation time 15 minutes
Cooking time 12 minutes

1 cup rice flour
⅔ cup potato flour
1 teaspoon xanthan gum
1 teaspoon gluten-free baking powder
1 teaspoon baking soda
6 tablespoons butter, cubed
¼ cup pitted green olives, chopped
4 sun-dried tomatoes, chopped
1 tablespoon chopped fresh parsley
1 large egg, beaten
4 tablespoons buttermilk, plus a little
   extra for brushing

Nutritional information:
Cal 198 (828 kJ) Protein 5 g Carb 21 g
Fat 10 g Saturated fat 6 g Fiber 2 g

1 Preheat the oven to 425°F. Place the flours, xanthan gum, baking powder, baking soda, and butter in a food processor and whiz until the mixture resembles fine bread crumbs, or rub in by hand in a large bowl. Stir the olives, tomatoes, and parsley into the mixture, then, using the blade of a knife, stir in the egg and buttermilk until the mixture comes together.

2 Tip the dough out onto a surface dusted lightly with rice flour and gently press it down to a thickness of 1 inch. Use a 2-inch cutter to cut out the biscuits. Place on a lightly floured baking sheet, brush with a little buttermilk and place in the preheated oven for about 12 minutes, until golden and risen. Remove the biscuits from the oven and transfer to a wire rack to cool.

potato and thyme griddle biscuits

These light bites are best served warm with some cheese or butter.

Makes 6 biscuits
Preparation time 10 minutes
Cooking time 5 minutes

1 large potato (about 8 ounces), chopped into ¾-inch cubes and cooked in boiling water for 10 minutes
⅓ cup rice flour, plus a little extra for dusting
pinch of salt
1 teaspoon gluten-free baking powder
1 teaspoon chopped fresh thyme
2 tablespoons buttermilk
1 egg, beaten
a little oil and butter for cooking

Nutritional information:
Cal 91 (380 kJ) Protein 1 g Carb 15 g
Fat 3 g Saturated fat 2 g Fiber 1 g

1 Place the potato and butter in a large bowl and mash together until smooth, then stir in the remaining ingredients until combined. Bring the mixture together to form a ball. Tip out onto a surface dusted lightly with rice flour, roll into a round about ¼-inch thick, and cut into six triangles.

2 Brush a griddle or nonstick skillet with a little oil and add a pat of butter, then cook the biscuits for a few minutes on each side, until golden. Serve with butter and cheese for a delicious lunch.

caraway and sunflower-seed rolls

Fill the kitchen with the fantastic aroma of caraway when you make these tasty rolls.

Makes 8 buns
Preparation time 25 minutes, plus rising time
Cooking time 25 minutes

1⅔ cups buckwheat flour
1¼ cups brown rice flour, plus a little extra for dusting
2 teaspoons xanthan gum
2 tablespoons instant dry milk
2 tablespoons sunflower seeds
2 teaspoons caraway seeds
¼-ounce package active dried yeast
2 teaspoons sugar
1¼ cups warm water
2 eggs, beaten

for the glaze
1 egg, beaten
1 tablespoon milk
1 teaspoon caraway seeds

Nutritional information:
Cal 220 (920 kJ) Protein 7 g Carb 43 g
Fat 3 g Saturated fat 1 g Fiber 1 g

1 Place the flours, xanthan gum, instant milk, sunflower seeds, and caraway seeds in a large bowl and mix together. Place the yeast, sugar, and water in another bowl and let stand in a warm place for 15 minutes, until frothy.

2 Pour the liquid over the dry ingredients with the beaten eggs, and stir together to form a soft dough. Tip the dough out on to a surface dusted lightly with rice flour and knead for 5 minutes. Split the dough into eight pieces and make each into a roll shape. Place on a baking sheet, cover with a damp cloth, and let stand in a warm place to rise for 40 minutes.

3 Meanwhile, preheat the oven to 400°F. Mix together the egg and milk and brush this over the rolls, then sprinkle a few caraway seeds on top. Place in the preheated oven for 25 minutes, until golden and hollow-sounding when tapped. Remove the rolls from the oven and transfer to a wire rack to cool.

blue cheese and rosemary biscuits

These are like a delicious cheesy pastry—great with cheese after dinner.

Makes 20 biscuits
Preparation time 5 minutes, plus chilling
Cooking time 12 minutes

¾ cup Stilton cheese, crumbled
6 tablespoons butter, softened
⅔ cup rice flour
1 tablespoon polenta
1 teaspoon chopped fresh rosemary
1 egg yolk

Nutritional information:
Cal 73 (305 kJ) **Protein** 2 g **Carb** 3 g
Fat 5 g **Saturated fat** 4 g **Fiber** 0 g

1 Place all the ingredients except the egg yolk in a food processor and whiz until well combined, or beat together in a large bowl. Add the egg yolk and whiz for a few seconds until the mixture comes together to form a soft dough.

2 Form the dough into a ball, then place it on a surface dusted lightly with rice flour and roll into a sausage shape about 6 inches long. Wrap closely and chill for half an hour.

3 Preheat the oven to 400°F. Remove the dough from the refrigerator, unwrap and place on the floured surface. Slice the sausage into 20 discs, arrange on baking sheets, and place in the preheated oven for about 12 minutes, until golden. Let cool on the baking sheets and then serve.

garlic and caramelized onion bhajis

These are great served with an Indian meal or filled
with your choice of filling.

Serves 6
Preparation 20 minutes
Cooking time 5 minutes

2 tablespoons olive oil
1 onion, sliced
2 garlic cloves, sliced
1 teaspoon cumin seeds
2 tablespoons chopped fresh cilantro
1⅓ cups gabanzo flour
1 teaspoon baking soda
½ teaspoon salt
1 cup water

Nutritional information:
Cal 310 (1296 kJ) **Protein** 10 g **Carb** 60 g
Fat 5 g **Saturated fat** 01 g **Fiber** 0 g

1 Heat half the oil in a nonstick skillet, add the onion, garlic, and cumin, and fry for 5–6 minutes, until golden and softened. Stir through the cilantro.

2 Meanwhile, mix together the flour, baking soda, salt, and water, and set aside for 10 minutes, then stir through the onion mixture.

3 Heat a little of the remaining oil in the skillet and add spoonfuls of the mixture, frying for 2–3 minutes and turning halfway through cooking. Cook the remaining mixture in the same way.

parmesan and paprika straws

These are fragile, but they are so tasty you won't be able to stop nibbling.

Makes 30
Preparation time 5 minutes, plus chilling
Cooking time 6 minutes

1 cup rice flour
⅔ cup polenta
¼ cup Parmesan cheese, grated
1 teaspoon paprika
8 tablespoons (1 stick) butter
1 egg yolk
2 tablespoons milk

for the topping
1 tablespoon grated Parmesan cheese

Nutritional information:
Cal 63 (263 kJ) Protein 1 g Carb 6 g
Fat 4 g Saturated fat 2 g Fiber 0 g

1 In a large bowl mix together the flour, polenta, Parmesan cheese, and paprika. Rub in the butter until the mixture resembles fine bread crumbs.

2 Mix together the egg yolk and milk, and add enough of this egg mixture to the dry ingredients to form a soft but not sticky dough. Form into a ball and chill for 30 minutes.

3 Meanwhile, preheat the oven to 400°F. On a surface dusted lightly with rice flour, roll out the dough to a rectangle approximately 1/16 inch thick, then cut into 30 strips. Place on a baking sheet and into the preheated oven for 5–6 minutes, until golden. Cool on the baking sheet, then carefully remove with a spatula.

caramelized onion and feta biscuits

Onion and feta are great together in these crumbly biscuits.

Makes 20 biscuits
Preparation time 20 minutes, plus chilling
Cooking time 12 minutes

1 teaspoon olive oil
1 small onion, sliced
6 tablespoons butter
½ cup feta cheese, crumbled
⅔ cup rice flour
1 tablespoon polenta
1 teaspoon chopped fresh thyme
1 egg yolk

Nutritional information:
Cal 63 (263 kJ) **Protein** 1 g **Carb** 3 g
Fat g 4 **Saturated fat** g **Fiber** 0 g

1 Heat the oil in a skillet and fry the onion for 10 minutes, until golden and soft. Meanwhile, place all the remaining ingredients except the egg yolk in a food processor and whiz until well combined, or beat together in a large bowl. Add the egg yolk and whiz for a few seconds until the mixture comes together, then knead in the onion until well combined.

2 Form the dough into a ball, then place it on a surface dusted lightly with rice flour and roll into a sausage shape about 6 inches long. Wrap closely and chill for half an hour.

3 Meanwhile, preheat the oven to 400°F. Remove the dough from the refrigerator, unwrap, and place on the floured surface. Slice the sausage into 20 discs, arrange on baking sheets, and place in the preheated oven 12 minutes, until golden. Let cool on the baking sheets for a few minutes, then transfer to a wire rack.

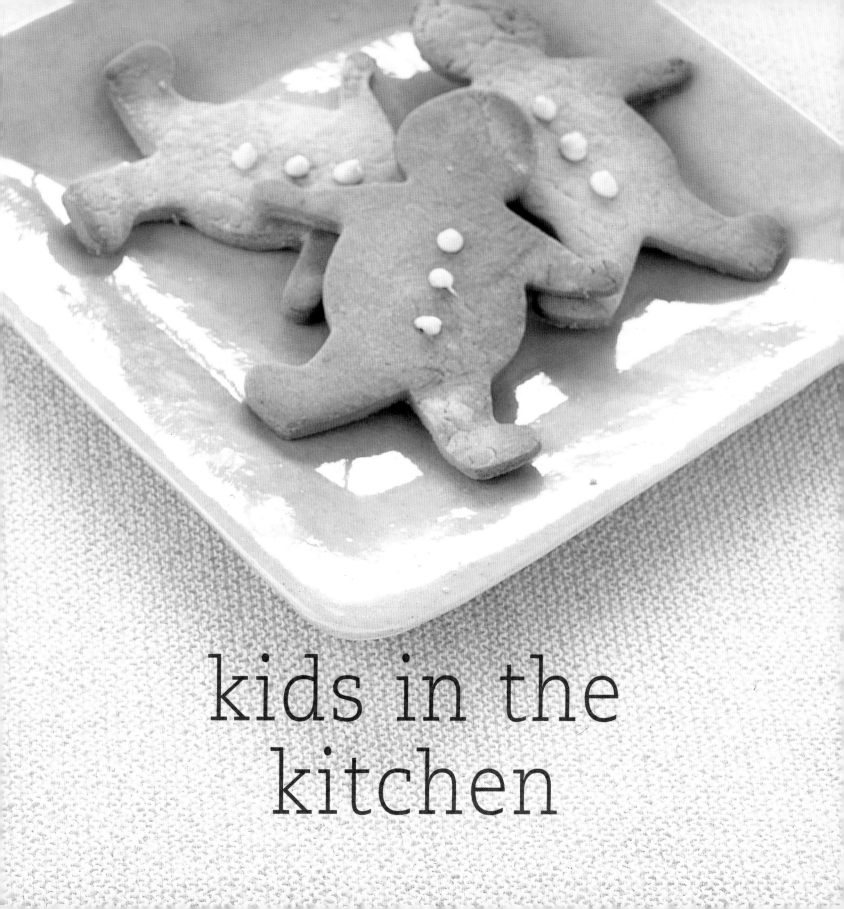

kids in the
kitchen

messy marshmallow krispies

Relive your childhood with these yummy yet oh-so-simple morsels.

Makes 12 cakes
Preparation time 5 minutes, plus chilling

5 ounces gluten-free milk chocolate
1⅓ gluten-free toffee bars (about 2 ounces)
2 tablespoons butter
½ cup dried apricots, chopped
handful mini marshmallows
2¾ cups gluten-free crisped rice cereal

Nutritional information:
Cal 122 (510 kJ) Protein 2 g Carb 20 g
Fat 4 g Saturated fat 1 g Fiber 0 g

1 Line a baking sheet with wax paper. Place the chocolate, toffee, and butter in a heatproof bowl over a pan of simmering water and melt.

2 Remove the pan from the heat, stir well, then mix in the remaining ingredients. Place spoonfuls of the mixture on the prepared baking sheet and let stand until it sets.

toffee crackles

These chewy nutty treats are great for a children's party.

Makes 12 cakes
Preparation time 10 minutes, plus chilling

2½ gluten-free toffee bars (about 3½ ounces)
⅓ cup gluten-free crunchy peanut butter
3 ounces gluten-free milk chocolate
2 tablespoons butter
3 cups gluten-free cornflakes

Nutritional information:
Cal 144 (602 kJ) **Protein** 3 g **Carb** 15 g
Fat 8 g **Saturated fat** 4 g **Fiber** 0 g

1 Place the toffee, peanut butter, chocolate, and butter in a small saucepan over a low heat and cook for 2–3 minutes until melted.

2 Remove the pan from the heat and let cool for a few minutes, then stir in the cornflakes. Spoon the mixture into 12 paper liners and chill until firm.

orange animal cookies

These crunchy tasty cookies hold their shape well
when cooked and look fun once decorated.

Makes 20 cookies
Preparation time 10 minutes
Cooking time 10 minutes

1¼ cups brown rice flour
½ teaspoon xanthan gum
1 teaspoon gluten-free baking powder
¼ cup packed light brown sugar
grated rind 1 orange
4 tablespoons butter
1 egg
2 tablespoons light corn syrup

for the decoration
1⅓ cups confectioners' sugar
1 tablespoon boiling water
food coloring (optional)
gluten-free candy decorations (optional)

Nutritional information:
Cal 106 (443 kJ) Protein 0 g Carb 22 g
Fat 2 g Saturated fat 1 g Fiber 0 g

1 Preheat the oven to 325°F. Place all the dry ingredients in a food processor, turn the motor on, then feed the remaining ingredients down the tube, adding a little extra flour if the mixture becomes too wet or adding a little milk if the mix is too dry.

2 Scrape the dough out of the bowl onto a surface dusted lightly with rice flour. Roll out the dough to a thickness of ¼ inch and use animal cutters of your choice to cut out 20 cookies, rolling up any excess dough and rerolling and cutting again.

3 Place the cookies on baking sheets and place in the preheated oven for about 10 minutes, until golden. Remove from the oven and transfer to a wire rack to cool.

4 Mix the confectioners' sugar with the water and add coloring if you want. Smooth over the cookies, or just use some to pipe on details, decorate with candy decorations, if using, then let set.

sticky
gingerbread

Adding preserved ginger to the traditional recipe
provides little jewels of surprise in this favorite.

Makes 16 pieces
Preparation time 10 minutes
Cooking time 45 minutes

2 cups brown rice flour
¼ cup packed light brown sugar
1 teaspoon baking soda
1 teaspoon ground ginger
100 g (3½ oz) butter
4 tablespoons molasses
2 tablespoons light corn syrup
2 pieces preserved ginger, finely
   chopped, plus 1 tablespoon of
   the syrup
⅔ cup milk
1 egg, beaten

Nutritional information:
Cal 139 (581 kJ) Protein 2 g Carb 32 g
Fat 18 g Saturated fat 7 g Fiber 1 g

1 Preheat the oven to 300°F. Grease and line an 8 x 6-inch cake pan. Place the flour, sugar, baking soda, and ground ginger in a large bowl and mix together.

2 Put the butter, molasses, corn syrup, preserved ginger, and ginger syrup in a small saucepan and place it over a low heat until the butter melts. Beat into the dry ingredients with the milk and egg and stir well.

3 Pour the mixture into the prepared pan and place in the preheated oven 300°F for 40–45 minutes, until firm to the touch. Cool, then cut into 16 squares. This keeps well for 3–4 days in an airtight container.

fruity biscuits with butterscotch sauce

Making these little biscuits is so easy, and they are loved by children and adults alike!

Makes 12–14 biscuits
Preparation time 10 minutes
Cooking time 10 minutes

1 cup brown rice flour
1 teaspoon gluten-free baking powder
8 tablespoons milk
2 eggs
¼ cup granulated sugar
¼ cup raisins or dried cranberries
1 tablespoon of butter, for frying

for the butterscotch sauce
4 tablespoons heavy cream
4 tablepsoons butter
¼ cup packed light brown sugar
1 tablespoon honey

Nutritional information:
Cal 166 (694 kJ) Protein 2 g Carb 24 g
Fat 7 g Saturated fat 4 g Fiber 0 g

1 Place the flour, baking powder, milk, eggs, and sugar in a bowl and whisk them together until smooth, then stir in the raisins. Set aside to rest.

2 Meanwhile, to make the butterscotch sauce, place all the ingredients in a small saucepan, bring to a boi,l and simmer for 3 minutes.

3 Heat the butter in a heavy-based skillet and add spoonfuls of the batter. Cook for about 1 minute, until bubbles appear, then turn over and cook for a further 20 seconds. Remove and keep warm on a plate while you continue with all the remaining batter, then serve drizzled with the butterscotch sauce.

victoria sandwich cake

This is a great everyday cake to which you can add flavors such as orange or lemon rind, if you want, or make a chocolate version for a birthday.

Serves 12
Preparation time 10 minutes
Cooking time 20 minutes

¾ cup (1½ sticks) butter, softened
¾ cup granulated sugar
1 cup brown rice flour
3 eggs
1 tablespoon gluten-free baking powder
few drops vanilla extract
1 tablespoon milk

for the decoration
4 tablespoons raspberry jam
confectioners' sugar to dust

Nutritional information:
Cal 253 (1058 kJ) Protein 2 g Carb 32 g
Fat 13 g Saturated fat 8 g Fiber 0 g

1 Preheat the oven to 400°F. Grease and flour two x 7-inch, round nonstick cake pans. Place all the cake ingredients in a food processor and whiz until smooth, or beat together in a large bowl.

2 Divide the mixture between the prepared pans and place in the preheated oven for about 20 minutes, until golden and risen. Remove the cakes from the oven and transfer to a wire rack to cool, then sandwich them together with the jam and dust with confectioners' sugar.

Variation

For a scrumptious chocolate cake ideal for a birthday celebration try the following.

Make the cakes above, replacing 1 tablespoon of rice flour with cocoa powder. Make a chocolate frosting by dissolving 2 tablespoons cocoa powder in 2 tablespoons boiling water and letting cool. Beat together 3⅓ cups confectioners' sugar and ¾ cup (1½ sticks) softened butter until light and fluffy, then beat in the cocoa mixture. Use to fill and cover the cake.

melting chocolate bites

Light and fluffy, these little cakes are also good for dessert with a little gluten-free ice cream.

Makes 12 cakes
Preparation time 10 minutes
Cooking time 6 minutes

3 ounces gluten-free milk chocolate
7 tablespoons butter
2 eggs
2 egg yolks
¼ cup granulated sugar
1 tablespoon rice flour

Nutritional information:
Cal 130 (543 kJ) **Protein** 2 g **Carb** 8 g
Fat 10 g **Saturated fat** 6 g **Fiber** 0 g

1 Preheat the oven to 400°F. Line a 12-hole mini-muffin pan with paper liners. Place the chocolate and butter in a heatproof bowl over a pan of simmering water and melt.

2 In a separate bowl, whisk together the eggs, yolks, and the sugar until thick and pale. Fold in the chocolate mixture and the flour, then pour the mixture into the paper liners. Place in the preheated oven for 6 minutes. Remove the cakes from the oven and transfer to a wire rack to cool.

chocolate and fudge mini muffins

These scrummy mouthfuls contain everyone's favorite flavors.

Makes 40 muffins
Preparation time 30 minutes
Cooking time 15 minutes

1¼ cups brown rice flour
2 tablespoons gabanzo flour
1 teaspoon baking soda
2 teaspoons gluten-free baking powder
½ teaspoon xanthan gum
½ cup granulated sugar
6 tablespoons butter, melted
1 egg, beaten
1 cup buttermilk
3 ounces gluten-free milk chocolate chips or chopped, gluten-free milk chocolate

for the fudge
13-ounce can condensed milk
⅔ cup milk
2 cups packed light brown sugar
7 tablespoons butter

Nutritional information:
Cal 71 (297 kJ) **Protein** 0 g **Carb** 11 g
Fat 3 g **Saturated fat** 2 g **Fiber** 0 g

1 To make the fudge, place all the ingredients in a heavy-based saucepan and heat gently until the sugar has dissolved; bring to a boil and boil for about 10 minute,s until the mixture reaches 230°F on a sugar thermometer. Remove from the heat and beat for 5 minutes, then pour into a pan and set aside to cool.

2 Meanwhile, preheat the oven to 400°F. Line four 12-hole mini-muffin tins with 40 paper liners. Sift the flours, baking soda, baking powder, and xanthan gum together into a large bowl, then stir in the sugar.

3 In a separate bowl, mix together the, butter, egg, and buttermilk. Gently combine the dry and wet ingredients, and lightly fold in the fudge, roughly chopped, and the chocolate into the mixture, stirring well.

4 Spoon the mixture into the paper liners and place in the preheated oven for 15 minutes, until golden and risen. Remove the cakes from the oven and transfer to a wire rack to cool. They are best eaten the same day.

fruity mango bars

Chewy and fruity, these are great for school lunch boxes.

Makes 12 pieces
Preparation time 10 minutes
Cooking time 30 minutes

½ cup packed light brown sugar
10 tablespoons (1¼ sticks) butter
2 tablespoons light corn syrup
5 cups millet flakes
2 tablespoons mixed seeds, such as
   pumpkin and sunflower
½ cup dried mango or apricots, roughly
   chopped

Nutritional information:
Cal 219 (915 kJ) Protein 3 g Carb 23 g
Fat 13 g Saturated fat 7 g Fiber 2 g

1 Preheat the oven to 300°F. Place the sugar, butter, and corn syrup in a heavy-based saucepan and heat until melted, then stir in the remaining ingredients.

2 Spoon the mixture into an 11 x 7-inch nonstick baking pan, press down lightly, and place in the preheated oven for 30 minutes. Mark to divide into 12 bars, then cool before removing from the pan.

marble cake squares

Vanilla and chocolate are common choices for a marble cake, but food coloring also looks great!

Makes 16 pieces
Preparation time 10 minutes
Cooking time 25 minutes

¾ cup (1½ sticks) butter, softened
¾ cup granulated sugar
⅔ cup brown rice flour
½ cup corn flour
3 eggs
1 tablespoon gluten-free
  baking powder
few drops vanilla extract
1 tablespoon milk
1 tablespoon cocoa powder

Nutritional information:
Cal 179 (748 kJ) Protein 1 g Carb 21 g
Fat 10 g Saturated fat 6 g Fiber 0 g

1 Preheat the oven to 400°F. Grease and flour a 7-inch, square cake pan. Place all the ingredients except the cocoa in a food processor and whiz until smooth, or beat together in a large bowl.

2 Divide the mixture in two and beat the cocoa powder (or some food coloring) into one half. Spoon the mixes into a bowl and give a gentle swirl, then spoon into the prepared pan.

3 Place in the preheated oven for 25 minutes, or until just firm to the touch. Remove the cake from the oven, let cool in the pan, then cut into 16 squares.

white chocolate drops

These cookies are so melt-in-the-mouth
they won't last long!

Makes 20 cookies

Preparation time 10 minutes, plus
chilling

Cooking time 20 minutes

¼ **cup shortening**

4 **tablespoons butter**

¼ **cup granulated sugar**

1 **egg yolk**

1¼ **cups brown rice flour, plus
extra for dusting**

1 **tablespoon ground almonds**

2 **ounces gluten-free white chocolate,
grated**

Nutritional information:

Cal 98 (410 kJ) Protein 0 g Carb 13 g
Fat 5 g Saturated fat 3 g Fiber 0 g

1 Place the shortening, butter, and sugar in a large bowl and
beat together, then beat in the egg yolk followed by the
remaining ingredients. Form the dough into a ball, wrap closely,
and chill for 1 hour.

2 Preheat the oven to 350°F. Remove the dough from the
refrigerator, unwrap, and place on a surface dusted lightly
with rice flour. Knead the dough a little to soften it, then divide
into 20 balls.

3 Place the balls on two baking sheets, flatten them slightly with
a fork, and place in the preheated oven for about 20 minutes,
until golden. Remove the cookies from the oven and transfer to a
wire rack to cool.

passion cake squares

Deliciously moist and full of wonderful flavors—
what could be nicer?

Makes 16 pieces
Preparation time 10 minutes
Cooking time 1 hour

1 cup brown rice flour
1½ cups granulated sugar
2 teaspoons gluten-free baking powder
1 teaspoon xanthan gum
1 teaspoon ground cinnamon
⅔ cup or corn oil
2 eggs, beaten
few drops vanilla extract
4–5 medium carrots (about 12 ounces),
   grated
½ cup shredded coconut
⅓ cup canned crushed pineapple,
   drained
¼ cup golden raisins

for the topping
1 cup cream cheese
2 tablespoons clear honey
½ cup walnuts, chopped (optional)

Nutritional information:
Cal 307 (1,283 kJ) Protein 2 g Carb 27 g
Fat 21 g Saturated fat 7 g Fiber 1 g

1 Preheat the oven to 350°F. Grease and flour an 8-inch, square cake pan. Sift the flour, sugar, baking powder, xanthan gum, and cinnamon together into a large bowl. Add the oil, eggs, and vanilla extract and beat well.

2 Fold in the carrots, coconut, pineapple, and golden raisins, and spoon the mixture into the prepared pan. Place in the preheated oven for about 1 hour, or until a skewer inserted in the middle comes out clean. Remove from the oven and cool in the pan.

3 Beat together the cream cheese and honey, and smooth over the cake, then sprinkle the nuts, if using, on top. Cut into 16 squares.

gingerbread men

A chapter for children would be incomplete without these friendly spicy characters!

Makes 6 gingerbread men
Preparation time 15 minutes
Cooking time 10 minutes

1 cup brown rice flour
2 tablespoons cornstarch
pinch of baking soda
1 teaspoon ground ginger
½ teaspoon xanthan gum
3 tablespoons butter
2 tablespoons soft light brown sugar
2 tablespoons light corn syrup

for the decoration
3½ ounces gluten-free white chocolate, melted
gluten-free candies or raisins (optional)

Nutritional information:
Cal 169 (706 kJ) Protein 0 g Carb 31 g
Fat 6 g Saturated fat 4 g Fiber 0 g

SHOWN ON PAGES 116–117

1 Preheat the oven to 375°F. Sift all the dry ingredients together into a large bowl. Place the butter, sugar, and corn syrup in a small saucepan and heat gently until melted, then stir into the flour mixture and bring together to form a ball.

2 Place the dough onto a surface dusted lightly with rice flour and roll it out to a thickness of ¼ inch. Cut out six gingerbread men or other shapes (depending on their size) with a cutter, then place on a baking sheet and place in the preheated oven for 8–10 minutes, until golden brown. Remove from the oven and transfer to a wire rack to cool.

3 Use the white chocolate to pipe features, such as buttons, onto the cookies and decorate with candies or raisins if you want.

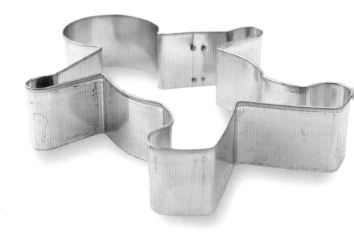

flowery cupcakes

Encourage the children to get artistic when decorating these scrumptious cakes.

Makes 12 cakes
Preparation time 10 minutes
Cooking time 20 minutes

1 tablespoon milk
½ cup granulated sugar
7 tablespoons butter, softened
⅔ cup rice flour
1 tablespoon garbanzo flour
2 eggs, beaten
2 tablespoons ground almonds
1 teaspoon gluten-free baking powder
1 teaspoon xanthan gum
few drops vanilla extract

for the decoration
1¾ cups confectioners' sugar
1 tablespoon boiling water
colored icing (those that are in ready-
   to-use tubes are great)

Nutritional information:
Cal 227 (949 kJ) Protein 1 g Carb 36 g
Fat 9 g Saturated fat 5 g Fiber 0 g

1 Preheat the oven to 400°F. Line a 12-hole muffin pan with paper liners. Place all the cake ingredients in a food processor and whiz until smooth, or beat together in a large bowl.

2 Divide the mixture between the liners and place in the preheated oven for 20 minutes, until golden and risen. Remove the cakes from the oven and transfer to a wire rack to cool while making the icing.

3 Mix the confectioners' sugar with the water and beat to form a smooth paste. Spread the paste over the cakes, then decorate with the colored icing in flower designs.

cheese, corn, and bacon snack muffins

You could make these in mini-muffin size too—
perfect for a snack or as part of a meal.

Makes 12 muffins
Preparation time 10 minutes
Cooking time 20 minutes

⅔ cup brown rice flour
⅓ cup corn flour
2 teaspoons gluten-free baking powder
1 teaspoon xanthan gum
⅔ cup polenta
2 eggs
6 tablespoons butter, melted
1 cup buttermilk
⅓ cup canned corn kernels, drained
2 ounces Canadian-style bacon, cooked
   and chopped
2 tablespoons grated Parmesan cheese
pinch salt
3½ ounces Cheddar cheese, cut into 12
   cubes

Nutritional information:
Cal 160 (669 kJ) Protein 5 g Carb 14 g
Fat 9 g Saturated fat 6 g Fiber 0 g

1 Preheat the oven to 350°F. Line a large 12-hole muffin pan with paper liners. Place all the dry ingredients in a large bowl and stir them together. Place the eggs, melted butter, and buttermilk in another bowl and mix them together, then stir this mixture into the dry ingredients with the corn, bacon, Parmesan cheese, and salt.

2 Spoon half the mixture into the paper liners, add a cube of Cheddar cheese into each liner, then spoon the remaining mixture on top. Place in the preheated oven for 20 minutes, until risen and golden. These are best eaten on the same day.

date and apple crumble tops

These moist cakes have a delicious crunchy crumb topping.

Makes 12 cakes
Preparation time 15 minutes
Cooking time 15 minutes

10 tablespoons (1¼ sticks) butter,
　softened
⅔ cup granulated sugar
½ cup rice flour
½ cup corn flour
1 tablespoon gluten-free baking powder
2 tablespoons milk
3 eggs, beaten
2 dessert apples, peeled, cored, and
　chopped
⅓ cup dried dates

for the topping
pinch of ground allspice
3 tablespoons brown rice flour
3 tablespoons light brown sugar
2 tablespoons butter
⅓ cup walnuts, roughly chopped
1 tablespoon water

Nutritional information:
Cal 265 (1,108 kJ) Protein 3 g Carb 27 g
Fat 16 g Saturated fat 9 g Fiber 0 g

1 Preheat the oven to 400°F. Line a 12-hole muffin pan with paper liners. Place the butter, sugar, flours, baking powder, milk, and eggs in a food processor and whiz until well combined, or beat together in a large bowl. Fold the apple and dates in, then spoon the mixture into the paper liners.

2 To make the topping, place the spice, flour, sugar, and butter in a bowl and rub in using your fingertips. Stir in the walnuts and water and bring the mixture together, then sprinkle it over the top of the cakes.

3 Place in the preheated oven for 15 minutes, until golden and just firm to the touch. Remove the cakes from the oven and let cool.

popcorn clusters

Kids will love helping with these yummy treats,
especially scraping the bowl afterward!

Makes 24 cakes
Preparation time 5 minutes, plus
  chilling

1 teaspoon oil
2 tablespoons popping corn
4 tablespoons butter
1 tablespoon light corn syrup
7 ounces gluten-free milk chocolate
½ cup unsalted peanuts, roughly
  chopped (optional)

Nutritional information:
Cal 114 (477 kJ) **Protein** 2 g **Carb** 8 g
Fat 8 g **Saturated fat** 3 g **Fiber** 0 g

1 Heat the oil in a large saucepan. Add the corn, then cover with a lid and shake the pan; the corn will soon start popping. Carry on shaking until the popping stops, then remove from the heat.

2 Place the butter, corn syrup, and chocolate in a saucepan and melt over gentle heat, then stir this into the popcorn with the peanuts, if using. Spoon the mixture into 24 paper liners and let set in the refrigerator.

pizza scrolls

You can use any topping to suit your taste or whatever you have in the refrigerator.

Makes 8 pieces
Preparation time 25 minutes, plus proving
Cooking time 15 minutes

2 x ¼-ounce packages active dried yeast
1 teaspoon granulated sugar
1 cup milk, warmed
1 cup rice flour, plus extra for dusting
1 cup potato flour
1 teaspoon gluten-free baking powder
1 teaspoon xanthan gum
pinch salt
1 tablespoon sunflower oil
1 egg, beaten

for the filling
4 tablespoons canned tomatoes, crushed
2 cups grated mixed cheese, such as mozzarella and Cheddar
3 ounces wafer-thin ham, shredded
handful fresh basil, chopped

Nutritional information:
Cal 331 (1384 kJ) Protein 12 g Carb 48 g
Fat 11 g Saturated fat 8 g Fiber 1 g

1 Place the yeast, sugar, and the milk in a bowl and set aside for about 10 minutes, until frothy. In a large bowl, stir together the flours, baking powder, xanthan gum, and the salt.

2 Mix the oil and egg into the yeast mixture and pour this into the flour mixture, using a fork to bring the mixture together. Tip it out onto a surface dusted lightly with rice flour and knead for 5 minutes, adding a little flour if the mixture becomes sticky. Place in a lightly oiled bowl, cover with a damp cloth, and let rise in a warm place for about 40 minutes, or until well risen.

3 Preheat the oven to 425°F. On the floured surface, roll the dough out to a rectangle approximately 12 x 10 inches, spread with the crushed tomatoes, then sprinkle over the other toppings. Roll the pizza up from one long edge, then slice into eight pieces.

4 Place the rolled-up pizza scrolls, side by side, on a lightly oiled, heavy baking sheet. They should be pushed up against each other so the sides are touching. Place in the preheated oven for 12–15 minutes, until golden. Eat warm from the oven, one or two scrolls per child, depending on appetite.

index

acknowledgments

Thanks to my husband, Phil, the boys, Ollie and Freddie, and my willing neighbours for sampling all of the recipes and giving their positive responses.

Executive Editor: Nicola Hill
Editor: Lisa John
Executive Art Editor: Penny Stock
Designer: Miranda Harvey
Photographer: Emma Neish
Home Economist: Felicity Barnum-Bobb
Production Controller: Manjit Sihra